9th Grade
All Subjects
Workbook

BEYONDBOOKSLEARNING.COM

Visit beyondbookslearning.com for more resources and to learn about our mission!

Pleased with your purchase? We appreciate your feedback! Your reviews help our small business make our workbooks more effective and help others find them. Thank you!

Concerns? Visit beyondbookslearning.com to leave a message. We cannot reply to you on Amazon. Thank you.

Math

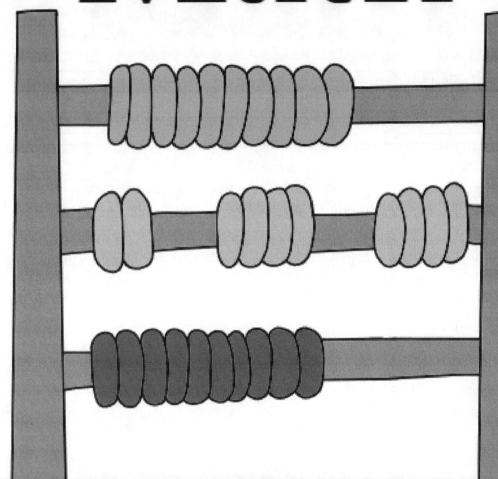

Factoring
Why should I learn to factor numbers anyway?

Sometimes, when learning new math skills, we ask ourselves, "Why am I learning this? What will I be using this for?" And, sometimes, why we learn these new skills and how useful they can be hasn't been explained in a way we understand. Factoring might be one of the skills you learn without knowing why you're learning it.

Let's talk about it.

Factoring is simply making complex expressions easier to work with by breaking them down into simpler components. After factoring, you still have the same quantity you started with, but now you can perform complex operations with them much easier.

Think of it like this: In addition, we learned that 3+4 = 7. That means, 3+4 is the same as 7. I could use one expression in place of the other, because they are equal. However, if someone asked me how many of a certain object I have, I would probably not reply, "3+4." I would say, "I have 7," because that is the most convenient way to relay the quantity in that scenario. But is that always the most convenient way to communicate that quantity?

When we are working with more complex operations, we always use what is most convenient to work with too. Once there are unknown terms or variables involved, it often becomes necessary to look at the quantity (like 7) in a different way.

This is done by factoring or pulling out similar terms to simplify. Factoring helps simplify complex algebraic expressions into broken down parts like 3+4 instead of 7. Sometimes pulling it apart a little helps us see what's inside. We can work with these "pulled apart" expressions to better understand how we can manipulate them in different operations. One way of simplifying is finding common factors.

Polynomials are a great example of something that is easier to work with when factored.

If you are wondering what types of problems can be solved by factoring, these include calculating area and volume, finding interest rates, and solving time problems.

The more you work with factoring, the better you will get at understanding and identifying patterns and the relationship between numbers. This helps level-up your math skills by leaps and bounds! If you can understand patterns and how numbers relate to each other, you can solve higher math problems with much more ease and confidence!

So, do your best at being patient while learning factoring, and remember that mastering this skill will ultimately help you in the long term.

Factoring

1. Factor this quadratic expression: $x^2 + 5x + 6$

2. Factor $x^2 - 4$

3. Factor $3x + 9$

4. Factor $6y - 12$

5. Solve by factoring:
Angela has 24 figurines she would like to arrange on her shelf in rows, with an equal number of figurines in each row. If she wants the maximum number of figurines in each row but more than one row, how many rows should she make?

Factoring

6. Factor $2x^2 - 7x - 15$

7. Factor $3x^2 + 10x + 8$

8. Factor $-6x^2 - x + 2$

9. Factor $x^2 + 4x - 77$

Factoring

10. The length of a garden is 3 meters more than twice the width, and its area is 90 m². Find the dimensions of the garden by factoring.

11. Factor $3x^2 - 7x - 6$

12. Factor $x^2 + 6x + 9$

13. Factor $10x^2 + 13x - 3$

Factoring

14. Write the correct terms for each part of the polynomial

Degree
Coefficients
Leading Term
Constant

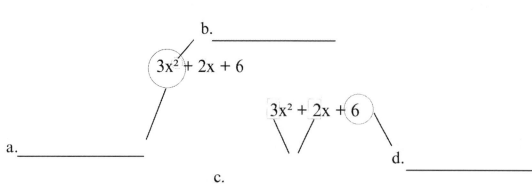

b._____

$3x^2 + 2x + 6$

$3x^2 + 2x + 6$

a._____

d._____

c._____

15. Which of the following are polynomials? Circle them.

$2x$ $2x + 2y - 4$

$3x + y$ x^2

$3xy$ $2x^2y$

16. Simplify $(2x + 4)(5x^2+2x-3)$

Polynomials

17. What is a rational expression?

18. Solve the rational expression $\dfrac{x^2 - 4}{x - 2}$

19. Solve the rational expression $\dfrac{x^2 - 9}{x - 3}$

20. Solve the rational expression $\dfrac{x^3 - 8}{x^2 - 4x + 4}$

Rational Expressions

21. Combine the like terms: $3x^2 + 2x - 5x^2 - 2 + 4x - 7$

22. Combine the like terms: $2a + 3b - 4a + 5b + c - 6$

23. Combine the like terms: $3(x + 5) + 2(x-4)$

24. Combine the like terms: $2(x + 3) -7(2x - 5)$

25. Combine the like terms: $2(3x + 4) - 2(2x - 5) + 6(x^2 + x)$

Combining Like Terms

26. Simplify $2^3 \times 2^2$

27. Find $\sqrt{81}$

28. Simplify $2^3 \times 3^3$

29. Simplify $2^3 \times 4^2$

30. Simplify $(3x^2)^3$

31. Simplify $\sqrt{225} + \sqrt{16}$

32. Simplify $4x^2 \times 19x^3$

33. Simplify $(19x^3)^5$

34. Simplify $(5x^3)^2$

35. Simplify $4x^2 \div 2$

Exponents and Radicals

36. Give the slope-intercept form of the equation for a straight line.

37. Describe each component of slope-intercept form. What does each represent?

38. Give the formula for the slope of a line.

$m =$

39. Give the equation for point-slope form.

40. Explain point-slope form and slope-intercept form and how they are used.

Graphing

41.   Give the equation of the line in slope-intercept form.

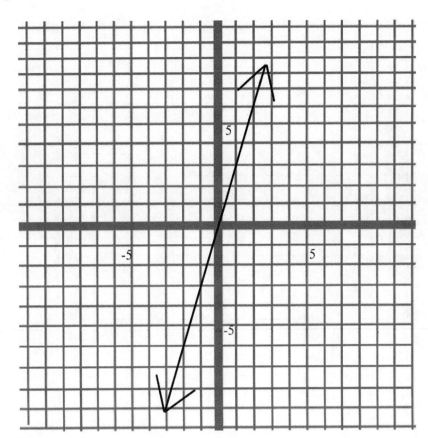

42.   Give the equation of the line in slope-intercept form.

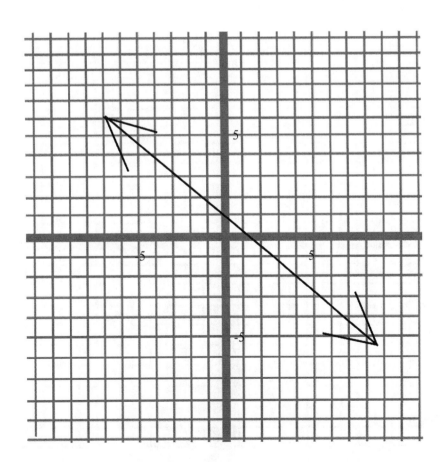

11

Graphing

43. Graph the following line: $y = 2x - 1$

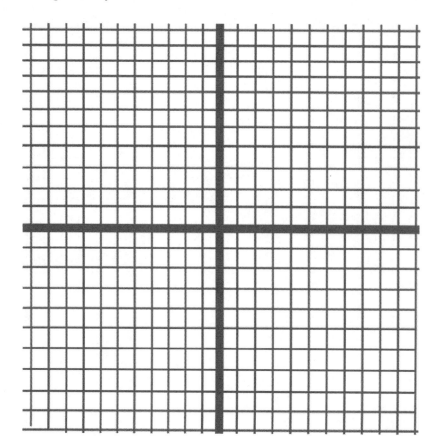

44. Graph the line $y = -x + 3$

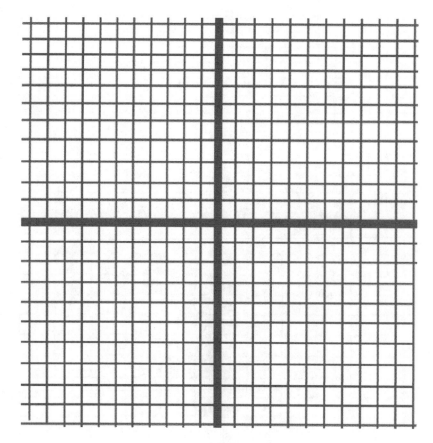

Graphing

45. Label the quadrants I - IV

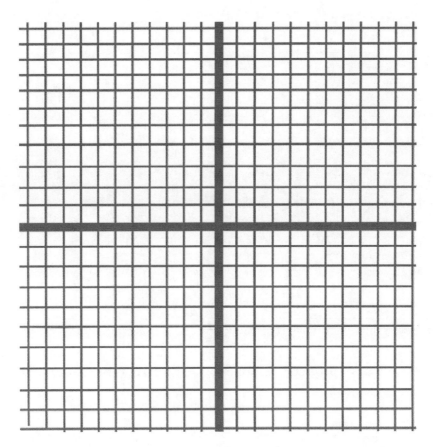

46. Plot these points on the graph: A (-3, 2), B (2, 3), C (0, 0), D (-3, -6), E (4, -2)

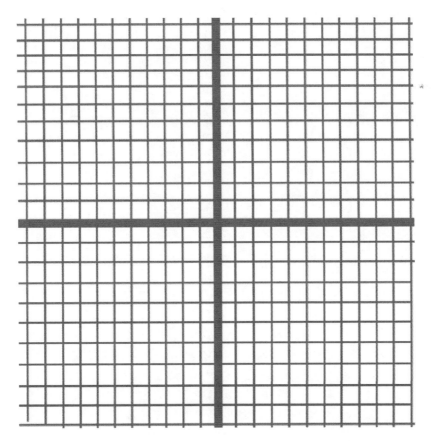

Graphing

47. A restaurant uses 4.5 pounds of rice per day, and they are open 7 days a week. How many 10-pound bags would the restaurant need to purchase to last 3 weeks?

48. You purchase a piece of property that is 90 ft × 1200 ft. What is the total area of the property?

49. The sum of two numbers, x and y, is 107; their difference is 75. Find the value of x and y.

Word Problems

Vocabulary

Define each word using your favorite dictionary or dictionary website. Make sure to note the part of speech (i.e. verb, noun, adjective, etc.).

Apex:

Atavistic:

Attain:

Autocrat:

Barter:

Bolster:

Bulwark:

Define

Use the vocabulary words in a sentence.

Example Sentences

Define each word using your favorite dictionary or dictionary website. Make sure to note the part of speech (i.e. verb, noun, adjective, etc.).

Burnish:

Chignon:

Coagulate:

Conscientious:

Contempt:

Crusade:

Denizen:

Define

Use the vocabulary words in a sentence.

Example Sentences

Define each word using your favorite dictionary or dictionary website. Make sure to note the part of speech (i.e. verb, noun, adjective, etc.).

Diaphoresis:

Disparaging:

Duplicity:

Enamored:

Erosion:

Fathom:

Fervid:

Define

Use the vocabulary words in a sentence.

Example Sentences

Define each word using your favorite dictionary or dictionary website. Make sure to note the part of speech (i.e. verb, noun, adjective, etc.).

Furl:

Gaunt:

Guild:

Harbinger:

Harmonious:

Humility:

Imperceptible:

Define

Use the vocabulary words in a sentence.

Example Sentences

Define each word using your favorite dictionary or dictionary website. Make sure to note the part of speech (i.e. verb, noun, adjective, etc.).

Impetus:

Ineffectual:

Interminable:

Irony:

Justifiable:

Laconic:

Malicious:

Define

Use the vocabulary words in a sentence.

Define each word using your favorite dictionary or dictionary website. Make sure to note the part of speech (i.e. verb, noun, adjective, etc.).

Maligned:

Melancholy:

Methane:

Morality:

Mutiny:

Naive:

Naught:

Define

Use the vocabulary words in a sentence.

Example Sentences

Define each word using your favorite dictionary or dictionary website. Make sure to note the part of speech (i.e. verb, noun, adjective, etc.).

Nomadic:

Obligation:

Patriarchy:

Predicament:

Prejudice:

Prodigious:

Prologue:

Define

Use the vocabulary words in a sentence.

Example Sentences

Define each word using your favorite dictionary or dictionary website. Make sure to note the part of speech (i.e. verb, noun, adjective, etc.).

Protagonist:

Reconcile:

Regent:

Relic:

Resolution:

Retribution:

Schisms:

Define

Use the vocabulary words in a sentence.

Example Sentences

Define each word using your favorite dictionary or dictionary website. Make sure to note the part of speech (i.e. verb, noun, adjective, etc.).

Scruples:

Serf:

Solemn:

Straggler:

Sustenance:

Taper:

Traitor:

Define

Use the vocabulary words in a sentence.

Define each word using your favorite dictionary or dictionary website. Make sure to note the part of speech (i.e. verb, noun, adjective, etc.).

Treacherous:

Turmoil:

Tycoon:

Unduly:

Virtuoso:

Vulnerable:

Zephyr:

Define

Use the vocabulary words in a sentence.

Example Sentences

Find the Vocabulary Words

```
H  U  J  F  G  X  W  F  B  C  S  S  F  U  D  O  O  P  T  P  E  M
Q  M  R  I  G  L  J  S  Z  G  H  O  X  E  B  I  M  N  J  R  N  D
R  V  P  Y  K  I  I  Z  K  E  O  E  L  H  R  A  D  M  B  O  T  L
X  Q  L  C  U  W  E  E  X  Z  P  U  A  E  K  V  H  P  F  T  B  L
B  J  W  S  C  J  A  P  W  A  G  V  T  L  M  Y  I  D  U  A  A  O
B  Q  T  B  A  H  X  H  C  R  U  S  A  D  E  N  Y  D  K  G  B  K
O  H  A  X  I  Y  A  Y  C  Z  L  T  Y  C  O  O  N  R  K  O  S  X
S  V  G  L  M  G  N  R  B  O  T  A  O  Y  W  Z  A  V  G  N  Z  S
L  Z  K  E  P  K  M  R  B  R  U  S  C  C  W  J  X  J  Z  I  M  L
K  I  R  I  E  U  M  Q  U  I  J  X  R  O  R  C  O  O  H  S  E  R
Z  Q  V  I  R  T  U  O  S  O  N  Z  H  G  N  A  H  K  I  T  B  D
M  T  K  E  C  E  J  Y  L  P  R  G  E  X  E  I  T  H  Y  J  M  Q
U  N  U  O  E  D  G  D  E  N  I  Z  E  N  L  S  C  S  X  S  U  A
E  E  A  G  P  G  R  A  X  K  E  T  H  R  E  S  D  Z  P  Z  T  T
U  C  O  N  T  E  M  P  T  T  S  S  O  Q  Q  L  U  Q  N  A  I  F
D  U  P  L  I  C  I  T  Y  H  U  T  S  B  M  G  R  Y  G  L  N  Q
Y  R  N  Y  B  M  G  Q  U  T  I  R  N  K  L  A  H  V  S  Z  Y  D
A  P  R  O  L  O  G  U  E  A  J  N  M  C  H  I  G  N  O  N  S  G
Q  S  Q  V  E  P  S  P  R  S  M  Q  F  O  W  N  G  Y  B  B  H  T
E  K  V  A  C  D  M  T  O  A  X  M  Z  N  I  D  Q  A  O  S  S  K
H  Y  W  D  W  I  N  X  S  H  W  E  D  T  X  L  Q  X  T  V  G  F
C  X  G  N  P  Q  X  C  I  S  E  J  Z  Q  D  V  O  T  C  I  L  Q
H  W  X  S  F  Z  X  E  O  P  I  P  H  K  I  P  U  E  U  J  O  G
F  T  V  S  Y  X  N  Z  N  Y  I  X  U  K  P  Y  G  A  N  H  P  N
T  T  N  J  P  B  P  I  N  A  K  Z  S  F  K  N  B  E  U  I  L  X
F  G  L  U  X  U  J  J  U  Q  M  T  M  M  G  L  D  W  I  F  L  Y
```

Apex	Erosion	Prologue	Zephyr
Autocrat	Fervid	Protagonist	
Bolster	Harbinger	Schisms	
Chignon	Imperceptible	Solemn	
Contempt	Impetus	Traitor	
Crusade	Laconic	Turmoil	
Denizen	Mutiny	Tycoon	
Duplicity	Obligation	Virtuoso	

Word Search

Vocabulary Crossword

Complete the puzzle using the defined vocabulary words.

Across

1. To reach, achieve, or succeed at something
3. To thicken from a fluid state
4. A desire to do bad
5. Nothingness
7. Bony or emaciated in appearance
9. Not having the desired outcome
11. To tell lies about someone or criticize them unfairly
13. Exchanging goods or services for other goods or services

Down

2. Reverting back to ancient ways
5. Lacking enough experience to understand the truth
6. Keeping a humble view of oneself
8. Filled with a strong feeling of love or fascination
10. Understand
12. Sarcasm, for one

Choose 4 of the previous vocabulary words to depict in a sketch. Place one sketch in each square.

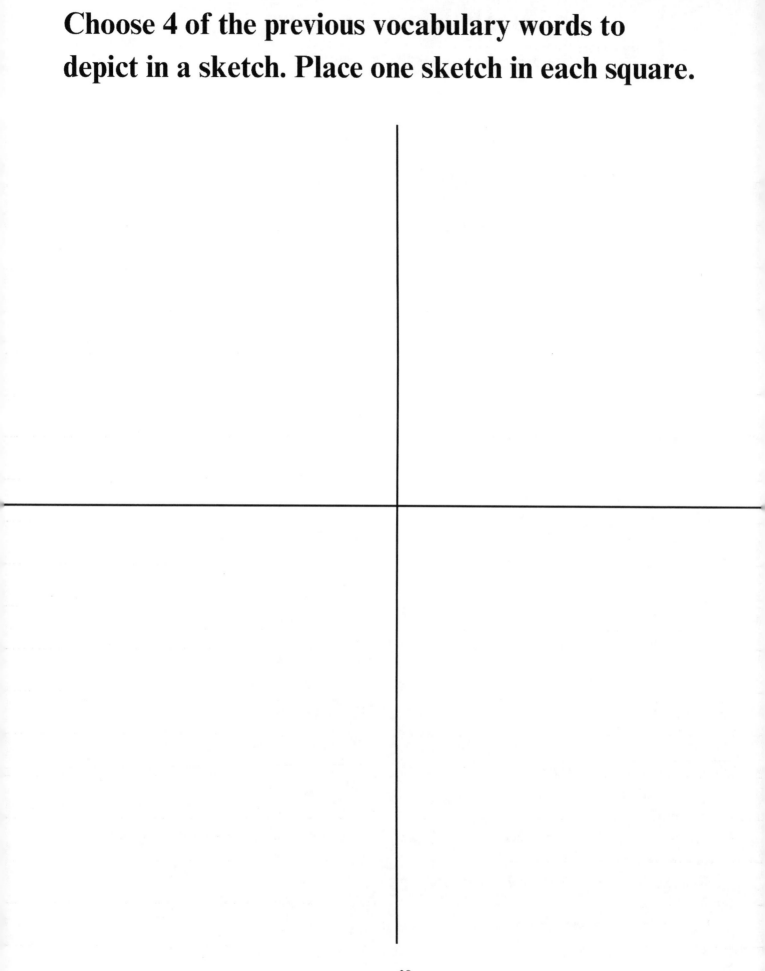

Sketches

Create a poem or short story that includes at least 5 of the previous vocabulary words. Be creative and use them in context to display understanding of the meaning.

Creative Writing

Creative Writing

Choose one of the vocabulary words previously defined and create a collage from magazine clippings, printed pictures, stickers, etc. that exemplifies the essence of the word.

Vocab Collage

Choose a movie, show, or book you have recently watched/read. Write a review using as many vocabulary words as possible while still making sense. Don't be afraid to get creative! Use extra paper if needed.

Write a Review

Create an article for a fictional newspaper in your town about an exciting upcoming event. Be as creative as you'd like. Include 5 vocabulary words. Use extra paper if needed.

Write an Argument

Writing

Dive Deeper

As you progress to more advanced reading levels, it becomes more important to be able to understand the intricate layers of writing. Understanding various writing styles and techniques not only enhances your comprehension but also enables you to engage more deeply with the text and share your insights with others. Here are some points to consider while reading.

Voice

Voice refers to the very specific and unique style or tone of the author. The entire attitude of the work comes from the voice of the writer. It is the same concept when we speak. We each have a unique voice. We choose the words we say carefully (hopefully) so that our listeners can completely understand us. If we are exceptional storytellers, we will be able to transport the person listening to us to wherever we need them to be by structuring the story in a comprehensive manner and using the best descriptions we can. We also try to engage our listeners by connecting with them. This takes tact on the speaker's part. We must know our audience. This is the same for our writing voice. Have you ever picked up a book and the words just seemed to flow off the page and into your heart? The writer seemed to know exactly how to speak to you. Chances are, you preferred that book because that author's voice was one you could connect with and enjoy.

Theme

The theme of a work is the underlying message being conveyed by the writer. It will often repeat throughout the writing. Themes usually speak to some sort of human condition. They are a commentary of sorts. They can be a commentary on the particulars of the story, or they can speak to humanity at large. For instance, the theme of a novel may be love in the broad sense or it could be specific to that character's journey with love. We can find the theme conveyed through the actions of characters, and by watching their development and experiences. These situations exist in the character's world for our benefit. Why? We should pay attention to recurring messages and concepts. Sometimes phrases or mottos will be repeated. Often, symbols and settings will be used to express a theme.

Themes can be tricky to find. It takes some time to look beyond the surface and see the deeper meaning. Sometimes looking at the writer's purpose will help. Why did he/she write this piece? What is the message? There will often be multiple levels and layers to a theme. Don't settle for the first and most obvious theme you see. Dig deeper. Ask yourself if there is a deeper meaning. Is there a greater purpose to this writing? The best way to do this is to relate it to your own life experiences.

Diving Deeper Into Writing

Figurative Language

Figurative language is one of the most exciting and artistic aspects of writing. This is language that goes beyond the literal meaning of the words. It often adds more meaning. There are various techniques in figurative language.

Allusion
An allusion is a passing and indirect reference to something without explicitly mentioning it. It will be mentioned in a way that will allow the reader to recognize the reference.

Hyperbole
These are statements of extreme exaggeration that are not meant to be taken literally.

Idiom
These are phrases that are usually specific to a region or culture. Someone who is unfamiliar with the saying would get a completely different impression of the meaning. The meaning is usually very far removed from the phrase. "Break a leg," means "Good luck!"

Metaphor
This is a comparison between two things that are not alike by stating that one is the other. "The car is a rocket."

Personification
Personification gives human-like characteristics to non-human things. "Whispering wind."

Pun
A joke that plays on the fact that a word has multiple meanings or that two words sound alike. "The duck said, 'Put it on my bill.'"

Simile
a comparison used to make a vivid description using the words "like" or "as." "He's as fast as a train."

Synecdoche
A component used to represent the whole. "There were plenty of mouths to feed.".

Literary Terms

What are literary terms?

Literary terms are words we have created to explain techniques and styles being used by authors and speakers to create strong works. These are the tools used to create a very specific effect for the reader or listener. Some of these terms include the figurative language we spoke of on the previous page. Here is a list of literary terms that are used often when examining literature. It's important to understand these terms and their applications to recognize their use and discuss the intent and meaning in a work. We can express our thoughts better when we can put our ideas into words.

Allegory

An allegory is a piece of work that has a strong visual representation of a moral or political message. The characters, places, and events represent key pieces of the message. "The Pilgrim's Progress," written by John Bunyan, is a wonderful example of an allegorical story.

Alliteration

Using words with the same beginning letter in close proximity. "Ally the angry alligator ate an ant."

Anaphora

Repeating words or phrases at the beginning of sentences. Do a quick search for "the most famous speech using anaphora," to see a wonderful example of this powerful tool.

Colloquiallism

Colloquial language is the language that is specific to a particular area or time period. A writer can use colloquialism to bring more authenticity to their writing. For instance, if a writer is creating a work that takes place in New Orleans, Louisiana in the 1940's, he would be wise to write dialogue between characters using the colloquial language of that time and place to create a more believable world in the work. Using words and phrases used in present day Australia in that work wouldn't make the story as authentic.

Epistrophe

Repeating a word at the end of sentences or phrases in succession. Search for, "Lincoln's Gettysburg Address epistrophe," for a historical example.

Erotema

This is a type of rhetorical question where the person asking the question expects a strong yes or no answer to strengthen his/her argument or statement.

Euphemism

This is a less abrasive, more polite way of saying something. "She is between jobs," instead of "She was fired for being late."

Foreshadowing

This is a technique where the author will hint at what will be happening later in the work. This may be used to create more suspense within the work.

Hyperbaton

Changing the order of words from the order the reader would expect to create an emphasis where desired. It will usually place emphasis on the first word or words in the phrase or sentence. "On the cold floor I slept."

Imagery

Descriptive language appealing to the reader or listener's senses.

Oxymoron

This is where contradictory words are used to describe the same thing. Example "Awfully good."

Paradox

A usually true statement that is seemingly contradictory.

Plot

A plot includes all the events in the story that keep it moving. One event will cause another event and so on until the entire story unfolds to the conclusion.

Point of View

This term usually refers to the perspective in which the work is written. Most works are written from either the first- or third-person point of view. Less often, a work can be from second person point of view. First person uses words like, "I," "we," or "me," whereas third person uses words like, "he," "she," "they," etc. In second person point of view, the writer will use the word, "you," to speak to the reader.

Soliloquy

A soliloquy is one character monologuing aloud to himself/herself. Unlike a regular monologue, the person speaking in soliloquy is alone and speaking to no one. This is commonly used in plays.

There are many more literary terms to learn about. The more familiar you become with these terms the more you can dive deeper into your reading and understand the intent of the writer.

Some classic literature that you can read to see many of these techniques at work include:

- **"Romeo and Juliet" by William Shakespeare**
- **"The Adventures of Tom Sawyer" by Mark Twain**
- **"Pride and Prejudice" by Jane Austen**
- **"The Call of the Wild" by Jack London**
- **"Frankenstein" by Mary Shelley**
- **"A Tale of Two Cities" by Charles Dickens**

Literary Terms

Abridged and Condensed

When reading older literature, it is important to understand that many books which have aged out of copyright often become subject to changes once they hit the public domain. When you purchase or borrow a literary classic, you may notice the words "abridged" or "condensed." There are subtle differences between these two terms but huge differences between these adaptations of the book and the original. We'll talk about what these terms mean.

Abridged

Abridging literally means shortening. If you think about a bridge on a road, it exists to shorten a drive that would otherwise route around whatever the bridge takes you across. Either way, the driver ends up at the same place.

This is exactly what an abridgement in literature does. Novels are long books full of plots, subplots, and figurative language that can be complicated to understand and take a while to read. When a book is abridged, many of the "less important" elements are removed. Subplots that can be removed without changing the main plot are taken away and many of the literary elements replaced with more simple prose.

This can help a complicated text reach more readers - especially younger readers who may otherwise struggle to understand the book. Elements that are seen as offensive in modern times or to younger audiences may also be removed or replaced with more favorable wording.

Condensed

A condensed version is similar to an abridged version in that it shortens the book. This version, however, breaks the story down closer to the bare bones. It squeezes out much more of the writing to get the story as simple as possible. Where an abridged version aims to simplify the story but keep more of the feel of the original text, a condensed version aims to get to the point of the story.

Abridged, Condensed, or Original?

The version you choose to read is completely your choice. It is worth noting, however, that many of the literary devices we learned about earlier will be lost to alterations. If you want to experience the full purpose of the work, the original version will be best. This comes with more complicated text, words that may not be used often today, controversial topics, and will take longer to read.

If you struggle to understand the original text, the next best option will be an abridged version. This will take less time and will probably sound more like the language you are used to. However, you may lose parts of the story and miss some of the key figurative language, but you will get a better comprehension of the main plot and message.

If a quick synopsis or overview is what you are looking for without investing the hours to read the lengthy full version, then a condensed version will suit your needs.

Choosing Literary Classics

Comprehension Tips!

What is comprehension anyway? Comprehension is a word you hear often in school. It simply means, "understanding." When it comes to reading comprehension there are two main types: word comprehension and language comprehension. Summarized, do you understand the vocabulary and the meaning of the story or text?

Here are some basic tools you can use to really level-up your reading comprehension game.

Build Your Vocabulary

Many students become discouraged when they read a text that has many unknown words. They believe that because they don't know the words (and therefore cannot possibly fully understand the text) they must be behind or inferior or (worse) not smart! This is not true! Think of it this way: when you were very small, you had to learn every word you know now. You wouldn't expect a one-year-old to understand what the word "tax" means. That's perfectly accepted by everyone. No one shames a one-year-old for this lack of understanding.

As you hit a certain age, you believe you have a fairly good understanding of language and, therefore, you must already know all the words, and if you don't you are just behind or inferior to your peers. Wrong! Building your vocabulary is a life-long process! You have to continue to learn the new words that come your way. How do you do this?

As you read and come across words you don't know, try to use context clues (or the words surrounding the unknown words) to figure them out. Also, write the word down so you can come back later to define it (or do this right away!). At the end of this writing section there is space for you to do this.

Keep building your vocabulary! The more words you understand, the better your comprehension will be.

Comprehension Tips!

Understand Your Purpose

Understand why you are reading the text. Is it to answer questions? Then you will want to know the questions you are looking to answer. Is it to summarize the text? Then create an outline as you read. Is it to learn a skill? Then you should highlight or take important notes as you go. Whatever your purpose is, understand that ahead of reading. So you know which strategies to employ.

Take a Peek

If you think diving in quickly and "getting it" makes you a better reader, you're wrong. Looking ahead and skimming headings and paragraphs is going to better prepare you for the text. Your brain will get into gear and be ready for what's coming. You'll also be able to organize your notes easier.

Take It in Parts

If you are reading a long text, it is best to break it down into more manageable sections. This will not only keep you from feeling overwhelmed, but it will also keep you on track to finish in a timely manner and to meet your deadline. It is important to stop after each section and assess your own comprehension. If you feel like you are lacking understanding, go back and retrace your reading to find where you are becoming confused. It will be easier to figure this out if you are periodically evaluating your comprehension.

Visualize

When you read something you enjoy, you naturally comprehend it better. You also naturally visualize what's happening. If you are reading challenging text or something you aren't as interested in, try consciously making an effort to visualize what is going on. It will help you walk through the plot and see a type of mental movie. This will help you keep characters and actions organized in your mind.

Try paying close attention to the news, online articles, advertisements, etc. Over the next few weeks, take note of euphemisms you hear or see. Write them down here as well as their actual meaning. Examine the list. Why do you think we use these phrases? Are there any recurring euphamisms? Why?

Euphemisms

Take a close look at the last book you read. Chose a character to analyze. What key role did this character have in moving the plot forward? What were the character's flaws? Did you like this character? Why?

Character Analysis

Character Analysis

Imagine you are at the beach. Write a short story about your day there. Use as much figurative language as you can to make the story very descriptive. Write in a way that places your reader in the middle of your story.

Descriptive Writing

Descriptive Writing

Descriptive Writing

Picture a mouse in your mind. Now make a list of 5 similes describing the mouse. Now make a list of 5 metaphors describing the mouse. Which seems to be stronger language?

Simile vs Metaphor

Imagine you have traveled back in time to the 1600's. You quickly become famous for your time-traveling claims. You are asked to write a descriptive piece explaining the future of society. Use the literary terms we learned (or others) to describe the future to the people of the past.

60

Descriptive Writing

Descriptive Writing

Descriptive Writing

Look back at the definition of an allegory. Write a short story in the form of an allegory. The message or moral can be whatever you like. Include at least two characters who represent key concepts.

Allegory

Allegory

Allegory

Story Arc

Let's talk about planning out a story. Many times, a writer will begin planning his or her story by drawing up a story arc. This arc is a graphic depiction of the main plot of the story. There may be subplots that do not fit directly on this graph, but this tool helps organize the key points of the main plot. The story arc includes all the major events that will push the plot forward. Most stories include the following points:

Exposition
This is where we learn about the characters, setting, point of view, etc. We are introduced to the story but do not yet know what kind of obstacles are ahead.

Inciting Incident
This is the event that introduces conflict to the story. The protagonist will need to deal with this conflict throughout the rest of the story. This is what begins the rising action.

Rising Action
This is the event that leads up to the climax. As the protagonist deals with the main conflict, there often arise other obstacles or events that stand in the way of solving the problem. These must be solved too as the story reaches the climax.

Crisis
The crisis is an internal conflict where the main character reaches a point of despair that seems unsolvable for a time.

Climax
The highest point of tension in the story - where the conflict and the protagonist come eye to eye.

Falling Action
All loose ends are tied up and unanswered questions are answered. Subplots come together and are resolved in this phase of the story.

Resolution
This is the conclusion of the story. We get some sort of (hopefully) satisfying glimpse of what the future will look like for the characters. We see the full picture.

Story Arc Terms

Many story arcs are depicted like this:

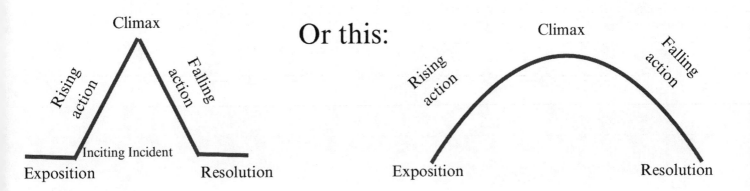

Or this:

This is a little misleading. In these models, you expect to see the climax midway through the text, with equal time for rising and falling actions. The truth is, the climax happens at different points of different stories. The arc can look many ways with exposition continuing throughout the story.

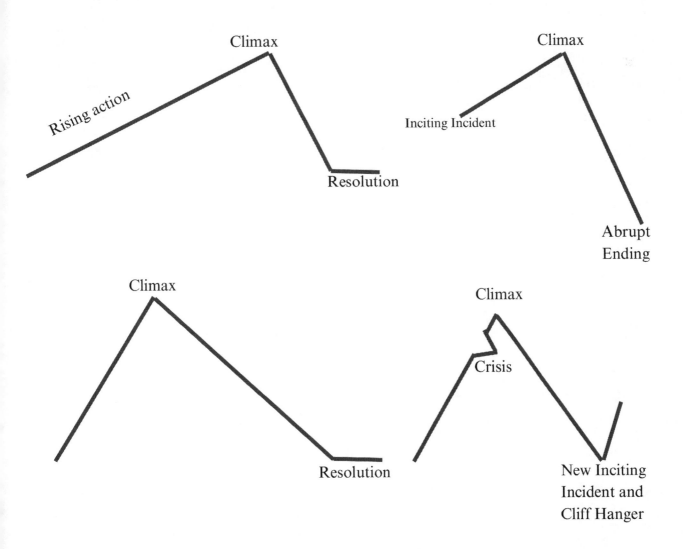

Think of the goals you have for your own life. Make a story arc of what you hope your life will look like from the months leading up to your birth until the years following your life and the legacy you hope to leave. What does your story arc look like?

Story Arc

Read the book "Alice's Adventures in Wonderland" by Lewis Carroll (1865). Graph the story arc below. Fill in the exposition, inciting incident, the rising actions, climactic event, falling actions, and resolution. If you do not have the book, check the library. If you cannot find a copy to rent or borrow, choose a book you do have and graph the story arc for that book.

Story Arc

Character Development

Most important characters will change in some way throughout the course of a text as a result of a conflict, relationship, or motivation of some sort. This is important for both the reader and writer to understand. The reader can understand the story better if s/he identifies the development of the character. It is the duty of the writer to make the character as authentic as possible.

Character development isn't just about the changes the character endures; this term also applies to the creation of a believable character. It is important that he or she is three dimensional. This means the character has to feel alive to the reader. This includes descriptions of flaws as well as strengths, mannerisms, feelings, thoughts, secrets, physical traits, personality traits, etc. It is the job of the writer to create something that feels within reach.

It is also important that this character has an arc much like what we saw with the story arc that described the plot of the story. This arc is called a character arc. Each main character (and some secondary characters) should go through a process of change. If the character stays unchanged, there usually isn't enough substance and intrigue within the story to grab the reader. Characters must face challenges and crises. They must be faced with hard decisions that speak to their identity. Try to get your reader to invest in the character's story.

It is acceptable to see the protagonist fail, but usually this is followed by a breakthrough. Whatever the arc, the reader must be able to follow the character's thoughts and see and understand the motivations and actions even if they don't agree with them. Without these elements, the text becomes unbelievable and weak.

Think of your favorite character from a book. What is that character like in the beginning of the book? What kind of conflict or challenge does s/he face? Does this change something about the character?

It is not always a profound change that occurs. The change may just be a change in perspective. It does not have to be a bad guy turning good situation. However, there is almost always some sort of transformation happening that leaves the reader with an emotional connection to the journey.

Character Development

Create a character born in 1899, somewhere in the United States. At the age of 25, this character finds a time machine and travels to 2024.

Build this character. Include physical description, strengths, flaws, personality, beliefs, health, etc.

Describe the reaction your character has upon reaching the year 2024.

Now describe the types of changes this character would undergo waking up back in 1924, suddenly. How would the character change from this experience? How would the actions of this person change? Personality? Beliefs?

Character Development

Write about a challenge or event in your life that changed your perspective or beliefs. How did this event change your character? How can you continue your journey of growth?

73

Create a short story featuring a character who finds a stash of millions of dollars in a deceased relative's basement. No one else knows about this money, so your character gets it all to him/herself. Show the development of the character through the story.

_____

_____

_____

_____

_____

_____

_____

_____

_____

_____

_____

_____

_____

_____

_____

_____

_____

_____

_____

Character Development

Character Development

Character Development

Words to Define

Word   **Definition**

Defining Unknown Words

Words to Define

Word   **Definition**

Defining Unknown Words

History

Why Do We Study History?

Could you imagine a world without history class? That would be one less class to worry about, but what else would change? What are we even studying about in history? If your answer is a bunch of people and places that are no longer around, you're missing the whole point!

Setting the Record Straight

Some people think learning about history is boring. The truth is, it can be ... if you're not doing it right. We, as people, are naturally curious beings. We like to learn things. Think back to when you were younger. Was there something you wanted to learn badly? How to ride a bike? Whistle? A sport? Why the sky is blue? Why hair grows?

We, as a society, must keep learning. Part of keeping forward momentum is understanding the past. If we allow ourselves to forget the history of mankind, we lose a record of our progress, and people begin forgetting. When we forget, we tend to repeat mistakes and lose certain skills.

Think of it this way: Why does a toddler remember not to touch something? Because that toddler doesn't forget the trouble they were in last time they touched it, the instructions not to touch it, (or worse) the pain caused last time s/he touched it.
If the toddler forgets the painful lesson of grabbing a cactus, he or she is bound to try again.
Not only does learning about history prevent us from making the same mistake twice, but it also helps keep track of where we are and where we are going. We hand off the information (hopefully) to the next generation to use.

Understanding the Fight

Unfortunately, a lot of our time in history is spent learning about war, because humans have spent a lot of time causing and fighting in wars. The war itself isn't usually the most important part of the lesson. Though we always have a great amount of respect for all who have fought in war, the important lessons for most of us come in learning what caused the war - or better yet - what could have prevented it and what happened as a result of it.

The causes of the war are important to understand so we can see what drove a group of people to that point. Was it a revolution? Was it political? Was it defending another country? Understanding what was gained and lost in the war is also very important.
From most war comes change. In that change come new laws and policies and either gained or lost rights. An important part of living as a responsible adult in this world is knowing and understanding your rights as a citizen of your home country and the world at large. You will learn how and why you gained these rights (and maybe which you have lost) by learning the history of your country.

So, as you are learning about history, ask questions and find answers. "Why did this happen?" "Why wasn't it different?" "Why did this group or government act in this way?" "How did this happen?" "Who was involved?" "Why were they involved?" "What did they gain?"

Learning About History

Being a Historian Means Being a Detective

Now that we know why we study history, let's look at how we study history. It is easy to pick up a textbook that includes all of human history between the two covers and think you know it all after reading it. Here's the problem: you are depending entirely on someone else's word on the matter. Someone else (or a group of people within a company) did all the work pulling that information together to give you a "comprehensive" lesson on history. The book might be a great book. BUT! The most important part of studying history is doing your own digging. We shouldn't rely on one source for information.

Studying history is like being a detective. We must look for credible witnesses and reports. We have to know the motives behind someone who is giving us information and where they found their information. We have to dig deep. The closer in time and proximity the source was to the event, the better. We aim never to take someone's word on the matter, but to find solid evidence.

Don't just stick to the main narrative either. Rarely is there one way of thinking. If you look back through science, for example, there are always competing theories until one (or more) loses momentum. Then, one theory becomes more widely accepted for some reason or another. The same can be true for history in some cases. There can be a widely held belief until more evidence comes to light and changes the minds of the people who study it.

Diving Deeper
Don't get me wrong, I'm not saying textbooks are bad. What I'm saying is, it is important to get more than one source for your information. It is also important to do research. Research is key. A textbook usually aims to summarize what the writer believes to be the most important parts of a subject, but they rarely give the entire picture and often skip the less common beliefs of the time. It is impossible to get all the facts and events of that subject into one book. In the process of summary, things can become lost.

Diving deeper into a subject you find important is wonderful. Collect more books on the matter. Look for primary sources from the time such as diaries, newspapers, era documents, eye-witness accounts, interviews, etc.
When you are searching online, take a look at the website. Who is running it? Is it an organization? Is it a credible organization? Is it a blog? Who is writing? What are the motives of the writer? Could they be considered an expert on the subject? Is the person credible? Is there persuasive language (more on this in the 10th Grade Workbook)?

Alway measure the summary you read against the primary sources you find and ask yourself if they match up. Is the lesson being taught matching the evidence being found? Now you're thinking like a detective.

In this section, you will be the detective.

Thinking Like a Detective

What's In a Century?

A century is a period of 100 years. But did you ever notice that the century is always 1 unit ahead of what you would think? For instance, we are living in the 21st century, but we are counting years in the 2,000's. And in the 2,100's it will be the 22nd century. It can be a little confusing, but there is an easy explanation. If you go all the way back to the 1st century, you find yourself in the years 0 C.E. (A.D.) - 100 C.E. This was the very first century. The 2nd century comprised of the years 101 - 200, which was all the years beginning with 1. It works the same way in the B.C.E. timeline. So, you can see where the confusion comes from.

Below are events in history. Research the event and write the appropriate century the event took place.

1. Joan of Arc leads the French relief of the Siege of Orleans.

2. The fire that destroyed the Library of Alexandria

3. World War II

4. Christopher Columbus lands in the Americas.

5. Martin Luther posts his 95 theses in Wittenberg, Germany.

6. The Ming Dynasty in China comes to an end.

7. The first automobile was created.

8. Crypto currency was made available to the public

9. The British make their first settlement in Australia.

10. The Second Sicilian Slave War (Second Servile War)

Find the Century

Types of Government

There are various types of governments throughout the history of civilization. Here is a list of some of the most common types.

Anarchy: Anarcy is more like the absence of a government. People within an anarchy choose whether or not to cooperate within society without a formal government leading.

Aristocracy: An aristocracy is a form of government that is governed by a small group of wealthy nobles who were considered, "the best" of society.

Confederacy: A confederacy is a group of people or countries joined together for a common purpose. The confederacy unites for a common purpose with a common government, but each group still retains some amount of autonomy. The common government between groups does not overrule each individual government. Power stays within the states.

Democracy: There are multiple types of democracy, but the common thread between each type is that the people hold the power. The government is in place to serve the people - not the other way around. In its purest form, there is **direct democracy**, where the people vote and decide on policies. This is a "majority rule" model.
There is also **representative democracy** where the people regularly vote for representatives to represent the interests of the people who vote for them.
There is also a **constitutional democracy** where the democratic process is ruled by the constitution of the country. The constitution has the final say on all matters. There are many other types of democracy as well, but the important thing to remember for each type is that the people of the country hold the power.

Dictatorship: In a dictatorship, there is one person who has nearly full control over the government without the consent of the governed.

Federalist: Federalism is similar to a **confederacy** in that they both have an overarching government and smaller governments governing the individual states. However, in a federalist nation, the federal government holds more power than in a confederacy. Power is held both at the state and national level.

Monarchy: A monarchy is also a government where one person reigns (such as a king or queen). However, in this form of government, the ruler often inherits his/her position. This is not typically like a **dictatorship**, because the king or queen is usually only the head of the state and not the head of the government itself such as in a **constitutional monarchy**. However, in the case of an **absolute monarchy** the monarch would have full power.

Oligarchy: An oligarchy is similar to an **aristocracy** in that both forms of government are controlled by a small portion of the wealthy population. However, in an oligarchy, the oligarchs are the ones in control. These are very wealthy businesspeople who influence the political landscape. These people control the majority with full political power, passing laws and policies in favor of their own class.

Socialism: Socialism is based on the idea of the community (or citizens) owning and regulating property and resources equally. This is not a form of government as much as an economic system. However, it does have close ties to the policies within the government. Ideally, each person is compensated according to his/her contribution. **Communism** is a subset of socialism where the property and resources are owned and controlled by the state rather than the citizens. Ideally, each person is compensated according to their abilities and needs.
It is typically believed that a socialist nation will lead to a totalitarian government.

Totalitarian: A totalitarian government is a centralized government run by a single person in a **dictatorship**. It is generally understood that a totalitarian dictator is more oppressive than a typical dictator. This leader exercises overbearing power by regulating nearly all aspects of public and private life.

Types of Government

Give examples of each type of government throughout history. Note that countries go through changes in government over time, so answers can vary.

Aristocracy:

Communist:

Monarchy:

Democracy:

Federalist:

Totalitarian:

Oligarchy:

Types of Government

The following pages include research prompts which will give you a history topic to research and investigate using your detective skills. Remember to look for reputable sources and write them down.

These exercises will require you to formulate your own thoughts and opinions based on the qualified information you find. Draw your own conclusions about the events based on the facts you find.

You will be writing an essay for each prompt. Use the pages provided to organize your notes. Dates, people, and events are important, but remember to think about the, "why" for each situation. Figure out why the events unfolded the way they did. Understand what happened and why. That's more important than reciting dates.

Ancient Egypt

Investigate the fall of ancient Egypt. What do you believe was the decisive blow to this great civilization? Give specific examples and evidence to support your theory.

Things to consider in your research:

Who were the ancient Egyptians?

When was this civilization at its peak?

What were some of the biggest obstacles and challenges this civilization faced?

Who were some of the forces who sought to conquer the area?

Were there any inherent environmental challenges to living in this area of the world?

Were there any social changes happening which may have weakened the society or divided it?

What was the political landscape?

Ancient Egypt

Keep a timeline of the events you find.

Ancient Egypt

Mesoamerican Civilization

Explore the Aztec, Mayan, and Incan civilizations so that you can write about the similarities and differences between their social and political structures, religious beliefs and practices, and achievements. Consider the variables that impacted each culture such as geography, environment, and complex historical events. Think about how these variables affected each civilization's development and decline.

Mesoamerica

Things to consider in your research:

What did the political structures of each civilization look like?

Where was each civilization located?

What were the unique challenges in each geographical location? What were the advantages?

How did each group practice religion? Did they worship one god or multiple? Did they share gods?

What type of technology did these civilizations have?

Did any of these civilizations have written languages?

Did they farm?

Did they face any common enemies or invaders?

Mesoamerica

Keep a timeline of the events you find.

Mesoamerica

European Exploration

Take a look at European explorers such as Christopher Columbus, Vasco da Gama, Ferdinand Magellan, and Amerigo Vespucci and their contributions to history. Investigate and identify the key motives behind the exploration of the world by the European governments funding these trips. How do these motivating factors contrast with the effects of exploration on indigenous cultures? What effect do these historic endeavors have on modern day global trade and economics, if any?

Things to consider in your research:

What is each of these explorers credited with discovering?

Which countries sent them?

What was happening in Europe during these time periods of exploration?

What were the impacts of these voyages and discoveries on trade?

Why would trade be a motivating factor in exploration?

Were encounters with indigenous peoples typically beneficial or not for the indigenous?

What were the effects of introducing new cultures on the existing cultures?

Do any of the effects of these voyages still exist? If so, which?

European Exploration

Keep a timeline of the events you find.

European Exploration

Joan of Arc

Study the life and actions of Joan of Arc. What is the significance in remembering her role in history?

Things to consider in your research:

Who was Joan of Arc?

When and where was she born?

What was her family's social class and standing?

What was happening in France during her life?

What caused her to support Charles VII?

How did she break gender norms?

What role do you think her faith played in her actions?

Joan of Arc

Keep a timeline of the events you find.

Joan of Arc

The Dark Ages

Research life during the "Dark Ages" in Europe. Choose a class in which to write about daily life. Pretend you are writing a diary from the point of view of a person in that social class (i.e. peasant, noble, clergy, merchant). Include topics such as housing, clothing, food, education, entertainment, family life, etc. What types of challenges and opportunities would someone in that class face daily?

Things to consider in your research:

What were the different classes?

What types of housing existed for each class?

What were the types of clothing available for the classes? Dyes? Materials?

What was the average diet at the time for the class you chose?

Did your class receive any formal education or training?

What kinds of financial opportunities were available?

Was social advancement possible?

Dark Ages

Keep a timeline of the events you find.

Dark Ages

Castles

Research castles in the Middle Ages. Learn how they were designed and why. What kinds of defensive features did they have in common? Investigate their significance and their role in society. What do you believe the castle symbolized in that time? Is the symbolism the same today? Why?

Things to consider in your research:

How was location decided?

How was this location and landscape significant to the blueprint of a castle?

Examine the duty of the walls.

What kinds of entrances were common?

What were some internal features?

How did they relate to economics?

How did they impact politics?

Castles

Draw a castle blueprint of your own using some of the features you learned about.

Castles

The Printing Press

Research the Gutenberg Press, invented by Johannes Gutenberg during the 15th century. What impact did this new machinery have on communication? What new capabilities did people have using this machine? Do you think this had any bearing on the Dark Ages ending? Why or why not?

Things to consider in your research:

Who was Johannes Gutenberg?

What did this machine do?

How was it used?

Why was this important?

What were the new capabilities?

What was used before this machine existed?

Who benefited from it?

What effects did this have on language?

Printing Press

Keep a timeline of the events you find.

Printing Press

Protestant Reformation

What is a reformation?

Now that you know about the Gutenberg Press, analyze the role of the printing press on the dissemination of Martin Luther's Ninety-Five Theses and other reformation texts. Explore the driving force behind the reformation and the authority the Catholic Church had at the time. What type of significance do you think this movement had on future generations, even up to today?

The Protestant Reformation

Things to consider in your research:

What was going on in the Catholic church during the 1500's?

Why were many Christians dissatisfied with the church?

How did nationalism tie into this movement?

How did economics play a role?

What did the printing press allow the reformers to do that they may not have been able to do before its existence?

What impact did the reformation have on society?

What impact did reformation have on politics?

Would Christianity have looked the same today without a reformation?

The Protestant Reformation

Keep a timeline of the events you find.

The Protestant Reformation

The Ming Dynasty

The Ming Dynasty in China was an era of great development in many aspects. Examine the art and literature produced in this period. What kinds of conditions must be present in a civilization to make advancements in art, science, and literature? How did those conditions manifest in this time period?

_____

_____

_____

_____

_____

_____

_____

_____

_____

_____

_____

_____

_____

_____

_____

_____

_____

_____

Things to consider in your research:

What kind of painting was prevalent from this period and area of the world?

What invention helped foster the art of ceramics during this time period?

How was furniture seen as art?

Explain the role of vernacular language in the flourishing of Chinese literature in this time.

What kind of political climate lends to advancements in the arts?

Do trade and exploration play a role in arts?

What was the educational climate in China during the Ming Dynasty?

Keep a timeline of the events you find.

Ming Dynasty

16th Century Russia

Explore the changes of the Russian political, geographical, and social landscape in the 16th century. Carefully analyze the role of Ivan the Terrible (Ivan IV) in these changes. What was happening to the majority of Russian citizens during this time? Were they prospering? What kind of economic struggles were the lower classes facing? What lasting changes did this period have on the country?

Things to consider in your research:

In what time period did Ivan the Terrible rule over Russia?

Did the Russian territory grow or shrink during his rule?

How did politics change under his rule?

How did serfdom affect the lower class?

Explore urbanization during this period.

How was religion affected during this time?

16th Century Russia

Keep a timeline of the events you find.

The New World Colonies

Research the migration to North America in the 16th century. Which European countries colonized this area? Where did each country lay claim and settle? Which groups of people were brought there as slaves during that time (indentured or otherwise)? Examine all these groups. What was the drawing force for different groups to travel such a dangerous and long journey to get there?

Things to consider in your research:

Examine the expansion on conquest from Europe into the Americas.

What were some of the reasons to flee to America?

Which areas did the different countries colonize?

Were the Natives receptive to the Europeans at first?

What is an indentured slave? Were any slaves European?

Why would someone agree to be a slave to get to America?

What influence did disease resistance have on the decision to use African slaves over Natives?

Keep a timeline of the events you find.

Spanish Conquest

Examine the Spanish conquest of the Americas during the 16th century. Pay close attention to the events that took place within the Incan and Aztec civilizations. What types of conflicts did the Indigenous people face with the Conquistadors? What other types of hardships did the natives face as a result of the explorers invading the lands? How were the natives exploited as a result of the Spanish conquest for resources?

_____

_____

_____

_____

_____

_____

_____

_____

_____

_____

_____

_____

_____

_____

_____

_____

_____

_____

Spanish Conquest

Things to consider in your research:

Where did the Spanish land?

Did they face any initial challenges?

Did the Natives attack the Spanish?

Were the Natives "savage" or did they have societies?

What kinds of hardship did the Native Americans face as a result of Spanish conquest?

Does this seem fair to you?

Why is the Spanish conquest of the Americas different than territorial expansion in Europe?
Or is it?

Spanish Conquest

Keep a timeline of the events you find.

Then vs Now

Look to headlines for current events in world news. Pay attention to the countries involved and the conflicts they face. What types of similarities do the world conflicts of today have with the conflicts the world faced in the events you studied throughout this section? Are there common themes? Why do you think these themes persist? Can they be resolved? If so, how?

Things to consider in your research:

Who are the main players in these headlines?

Which countries are involved?

Have they been involved in conflict in the past?

Has the political landscape changed?

Has technology changed the way we look at global conflicts?

Then vs Now

Keep a timeline of the events you find.

Then vs Now

Science

Earth Science

Earth science is a branch of science that studies the Earth and its various processes. Within the branch of Earth science, there are subfields that focus on particular systems occurring on, within, or around the Earth. Some of these subfields include:

Astronomy:
Astronomy is the study of objects and phenomena that occur outside the Earth's atmosphere.

Ecology:
This is the study of organisms and how they react with each other and their environment. This study includes the investigation of ecosystems and populations.

Environmental Science:
This is the study of the interactions between humans and their environment. Environmental scientists focus on subjects such as pollution, deforestation and other habitat losses, and climate trends. By studying these subjects, these scientists hope to implement strategies such as conservation efforts to keep a balance in the environment.

Geology:
Geology is the study of rocks, minerals, oil, gas, plate tectonics, erosion, and volcanic activity. Through geology, scientists can learn about the history of the Earth and the land formations. Geology includes its own subset of studies including:
- Paleontology
- Volcanology
- Seismology
- Geophysics   and more

Meteorology:
In this field of science, scientists, called meteorologists, study the atmosphere and weather. These scientists study the atmospheric temperature, pressure, humidity, precipitation, wind direction, as well as extreme weather conditions. These studies help us understand weather trends.

Oceanography:
Oceanography, as you may have guessed, is the study of the Earth's oceans. Oceanographers (scientists who study the oceans) analyze the physical, chemical, biological, and geographical characteristics of these bodies of water. Oceanographers pay attention to sea levels, marine life, and marine pollution.

Intro to Earth Science

Lab Reports

Every good scientist knows to record his or her findings! A lab report is the way to record findings during testing or experiments. This report explains everything from the materials used to the analysis of the findings. It's what the scientist uses to communicate what they did, what they expected to find, and what they actually found. Here are some of the key points you will find in a lab report:

Title:
Giving your experiment a title helps people understand what the experiement is about. The titles are usually descriptive enough that the reader can take a good guess about what to expect from it.

Introduction:
An introduction introduces an idea or experiment by explaining what it is all about. This area might explain why the study is being done and what expectations there are for the results or the hypothesis. A hypothesis is an educated guess about the outcome of the experiment. It is usually written in "If ..., then ..." form. For example, "If the temperature of the water is raised, then the rate of evaporation will increase." There is a condition (cause) followed by a predicted outcome (effect). The purpose of the experiment is to test the hypothesis. This is the common form of formulating a hypothesis, because you can easily see if there is a correlation. The introduction will also state the objective or purpose of the experiment.

Materials and Methods:
This is the recipe part of the experiment. All the things needed to perform the experiment are listed, followed by precise steps to conduct the experiment so that the experiment can be easily replicated.

Results:
This section shows what was found. This isn't a conclusion. This section just shows the findings. They can be written into words or shown as data in numbers, graphs, drawings, etc.

Discussion/Conclusion:
This could be one section or split into two. In these sections, the researcher takes the time to wrap up the experiment by discussing what was found, what was expected/unexpected, what could have been changed, etc. This is where the data is discussed and analyzed. What do the results mean? What does this information tell the researcher? This is the summary of what was learned.

This section includes experiments and areas to include data notes as well as a lab report. Do your best to analyze the results of these tests. What do they mean? How are they connected to every day observations?

Introduction to Lab Reports

Earth science is an exciting field that you are capable of studying easily on your own. In fact, you have probably been studying Earth science on your own since you were a young child. Have you ever collected rocks, watched the wildlife in a stream, collected shells and other specimens on a beach, examined the clouds, or compared leaves? This is the beginning of the study of the Earth. We all do it without even knowing. It would actually be quite difficult to be a citizen of this world without ever having observations about it. Once you begin to become aware of your data and its patterns, you then have valuable findings.

In this section, we will discuss basic Earth Science concepts. You will be given exercises designed to guide you in effective observations of models of Earth systems and processes. These exercises are curated to guide you into using your logical and critical thinking processes to make connections.

More importantly, these exercises should be a fun way to study the world around you. A good scientist is very much like a good detective. Ask questions and measure your objective findings against what you are taught to analyze whether or not they match.

You may have learned some of these concepts in lower grades. Your mission is to make connections from the exercises to the larger processes you see in the world. These are models that should represent what happens on the Earth.

Lab Safety

Lab safety is of utmost importance whenever you are working on tests and experiments. Not only does it keep you safe, but it also keeps the environment conducive to learning. Here are some important tips for safety during science lab experiments.

Safety Equipment:

Safety equipment (or Personal Protective Equipment known as PPE) is designed to keep you and those around you safe. There are some basic PPE items that should be on hand for a majority of your lab experiments. Depending on the materials being used, more specialized PPE could be necessary. When in doubt, ask a trusted adult for safety guidance and help. Here is a list of PPE you should have on hand for the experiments in this section:

- Goggles to protect your eyes from vapors, splashes, and hard objects
- Well-fitting apron or lab coat
- Fire extinguisher in working condition, ready to use
- Hand protection (appropriate gloves)

Ventilation:

Depending on the substances you are working with, ventilation could be extremely important. Always check labels of substances you are working with for ventilation warnings as well as procedures in the experiment. Remember, when in doubt, ask a reliable adult for guidance.

Organization:

Keeping a clean and organized workspace is important for safety. Clear unnecessary clutter to avoid accidents. Store all equipment, chemicals, and other materials according to their labels and instructions. Also dispose of waste according to the labels.

Safe Chemical Handling:

Proper storage of chemicals is important and so is proper handling. Always read labels and follow instructions carefully. Use proper tools to measure chemicals and wear PPE whenever appropriate. Even substances in your home you may not consider a safety concern such as vinegar can cause injury. Handle these substances carefully and use PPE to avoid injury or accidents that may cause fire or fumes. It is very important to never mix substances without consulting labels and an adult. It may seem innocent to mix two common substances, but they may create dangerous gases or substances when combined.

Be Prepared:

Not only should you have all materials ready for your experiment before it is time to begin, but you should also be prepared for emergencies. Make sure you have a complete first-aid kit, fire extinguisher, fire alarms, proper ventilation, proper cleanup materials such as paper towels or sawdust, a fan, open window, and other safety items nearby BEFORE beginning the lab. Always be aware of emergency exits and fire exits. Review this information together with an adult before beginning.

Hygeine:

It is a good idea to avoid eating or drinking anything while conducting a lab. As a rule of thumb, do not conduct an experiment near food or drinks. Do not bring food or drinks into your lab area. Always properly wash hands and clothes after a lab experiment. Keep hair tied back. Be sure not to wear loose fitting clothes or jewelry.

Be sure to conduct these and any other experiments with a trusted adult!

Rocks and Minerals

The Earth has many different rocks. If you step outside you can find a variety of shapes, colors, and textures in your own backyard. However, there are three basic categories of rock on Earth. They are:

Igneous Rock:

Igneous rock forms when magma or lava cools. These molten rocks cool and crystalize and can form either above or below ground. We can categorize igneous rocks based on their mineral content and texture. These rocks do not contain visible layers. **Intrusive igneous rocks** formed below the surface where magma cooled slowly, whereas **extrusive igneous rocks** formed above the surface where lava cooled quickly. Look up pictures of the following igneous rocks to get an idea of what they look like:

- Granite
- Obsidian
- Basalt
- Pumice

Sedimentary Rocks:

Sedimentary rocks form as minerals, rocks, and organic matter gathers and cements. These gathered substances are called **sediment**. They have gone through processes of erosion and transportation and have been deposited into a location where they undergo compaction and cementation where they form rocks. These rocks do contain layers. Examples to search and review online or in a book:

- Coal
- Sandstone
- Limestone
- Shale

Metamorphic Rocks:

Metamorphic rocks form when other rocks are exposed to heat, pressure, and/or chemical processes underground. These are rocks that have morphed into new rocks because of an outside force. The parent rock, or original rock, is changed by one of the previously mentioned forces to create a new rock with a new mineral composition and texture. These rocks may or may not have layers. Some examples to research:

- Marble
- Slate
- Soapstone
- Quartzite

Magma vs Lava

After reading the previous section on igneous rock, you may wonder what the difference between magma and lava is. Let's first talk about what they both *are*.

What are they?

Magma and lava are both types of extremely hot, molten or semi molten rock. **Molten rock** is extremely hot, melted rock. The molten rock is created through pressure changes, heating, and a process called flux melting where volatile gases contact material in the Earth's mantle.

What is the difference?

Magma is the term used for molten rock that is still beneath or within the Earth's crust. Magma is created in the lower crust or upper mantle of the Earth, but rises to the crust because it is less dense than surrounding rock. It has a lower density, in part, because of the gas bubbles that become trapped inside the rock.

The magma collects in areas called magma chambers and when enough is collected in these chambers, it pushes up to the surface. It can also rise through the crust when tectonic shifts occur.

Lava, on the other hand, is what the molten rock is called once it reaches the surface. Because the atmosphere is much colder than the molten rock, it begins cooling quickly, causing it to turn black in color, in contrast to the glowing red/orange of magma. When lava pushes forth from the Earth, we call this an eruption.

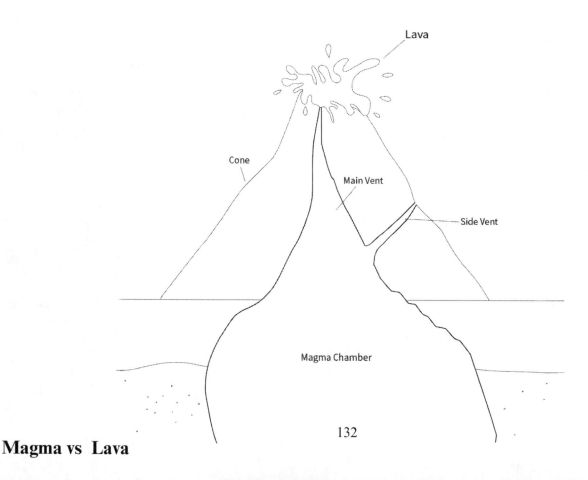

Lava

Cone

Main Vent

Side Vent

Magma Chamber

132

Try It Yourself!

Go outside and observe the rocks nearby. Do they all look the same? Which do you think are naturally occurring in that area and which do you believe were placed there for gravel roads, decor, etc.? Take samples from this area. If you have the opportunity to travel to a park, or other location, look at rock samples there. Are these the same? Compare the rock samples in multiple areas. Do they have anything in common? Characteristics to look for:

- Color
- Hardness
- Smearing (Do the rocks smear color when rubbed?)
- Magnetism: Take a strong magnet (a refrigerator magnet can work in a pinch, but a stronger magnet is recommended) with you and see which rocks are magnetic
- Look for layers of color or different texture throughout the rock. Which types of rock could these be?
- Use a magnifying glass to look at the structures more carefully.
- Notice whether or not the rocks are smooth or rough. If they are smooth, how did they get that way? What types of forces do you think caused the rock to become smooth?
- Keep an eye out for fossils! They can be found when you least expect it.

Some rocks are magnetic because they contain iron-bearing minerals! Sediments and soil can be magnetic too! Magnetite is one mineral that is quite magnetic (as you could probably guess from its name). Magnetite is an iron ore which is why it is so magnetic.

Did you know most meteorites are also magnetic? Wouldn't it be cool to find one of those! If you go meteorite hunting, look for rocks that are heavy for their size, will likely attract a magnet, some may have pits in them, and a crusty outer surface. These will not contain the mineral quartz.

Analysis:

What do the rocks around you tell you about your location? Do you think you have a lot of igneous rocks or sedimentary rocks? What about metamorphic? Are there a lot of iron-bearing rocks in your area? What do you think that means? Were you able to find a variety of rocks or were they all similar? Do you live near water where there are many smooth rocks? Did you see any rocks you searched on the rocks and minerals page? Did you find any fossils?

Try It Yourself Rock ID

Investigate the Effect of Magma Consistency on Eruption

Objectives:
To investigate the effects of changing magma consistency on the force of the eruption of a volcano. Will a more viscous "magma" create a larger or smaller eruption?

Materials:
- PPE (Gloves, apron, and goggles)
- Baking Soda (Sodium bicarbonate)
- Dish soap
- Water
- A cup
- Vinegar
- Funnel
- Plastic bottles
- Ruler
- Food dye
- Measuring spoons and cups
- A cookie sheet or basin tall enough to catch the liquids

Precautions:

Always wear protective equipment when performing science labs. This includes eye protection, gloves, and protective clothes over your skin. Do not let vinegar or baking soda sit on skin. Wash with water and gentle soap immediately. Wear safety goggles for this experiment. When in doubt, ask a trusted adult for help.

Procedure:
1. Equip personal protection equipment.
2. Place the plastic bottle or other small-mouthed container on the cookie sheet.
3. In your cup, add a couple drops of the food dye to 1/3 cup vinegar. Then add a few drops of water and a few drops of dish soap.
4. Using a funnel, add one tablespoon baking soda into the empty water bottle.
5. Quickly add the vinegar mixture and remove the funnel.
6. Observe and record the reaction between the dry and wet ingredients.
7. Repeat the experiment using various amounts of each substance. Record which combinations work best for the desired results and what kind of results you observe from each combination. You may also try changing the type of container you use. What is the purpose of the dish soap? Try this experiment without it. What is the difference between the eruptions with the dish soap and the ones without? Measure the height of the eruption to get a better understanding of the force of each eruption.

Analysis:
Analyze the data. Identify patterns. What are your findings? What is your conclusion based on this experiment? Was your hypothesis correct? What could have been done differently to make the experiment better? How do these findings relate to real-world conditions for magma and lava?

Earth Science Lab

Data Log

Earth Science Lab

Experiment Title:

Objective:

Hypothesis:

Procedure:

Observations/ Results:

Conclusion:

Earth Science Lab

The Effects of Temperature Changes on Sea Levels

Objectives:

To observe the effects of climate changes on sea levels by melting ice in a full glass of water. Will the glass of water overflow when the ice melts?

Materials:

- Tall Glass or container
- Water
- Ice cubes
- Tray

Precautions:

Always wear protective equipment when performing science labs. This includes eye protection, gloves, and protective materials over your skin. When in doubt, ask a trusted adult for help.

Procedure:

1. Equip personal protection equipment.
2. Place the glass in the middle of the tray.
3. Fill with water close to the rim but not to the top.
4. Add as much ice as you can without overflowing the water. Make sure no ice is hanging over the edge.
5. Allow the glass to sit, untouched, until the ice has completely melted.
6. Observe the level of the water once the ice has completely melted. Has the cup overflown? Why or why not? How does this relate to the real-world?
7. Record your findings and analyze the data. What could you have done to make this experiment better?

Thinking further:

Using what you learn from this experiment, you can see what melting ice caps can do to sea levels. But what about other frozen water sources? Are there sources outside the ocean that could melt and contribute to rising sea levels? How could you incorporate that into the experiment? Is this a realistic threat to today's climate?

To get a better understanding of the cycles of Earth's ever-changing climate, you can do some research on this topic. What kind of patterns do scientists see? What types of temperature changes has the Earth undergone? What kinds of changes in carbon dioxide in the atmosphere have been found over the past 100 years? What about the past 1,000 years? Beyond that? How do scientists measure these changes? Is this a reliable method? Do these trends point to human behavior causing these changes today? How can you tell?

Earth Science Lab

Data Log

Earth Science Lab

Experiment Title:

Objective:

Hypothesis:

Procedure:

Observations/ Results:

Conclusion:

Earth Science Lab

The Water Cycle

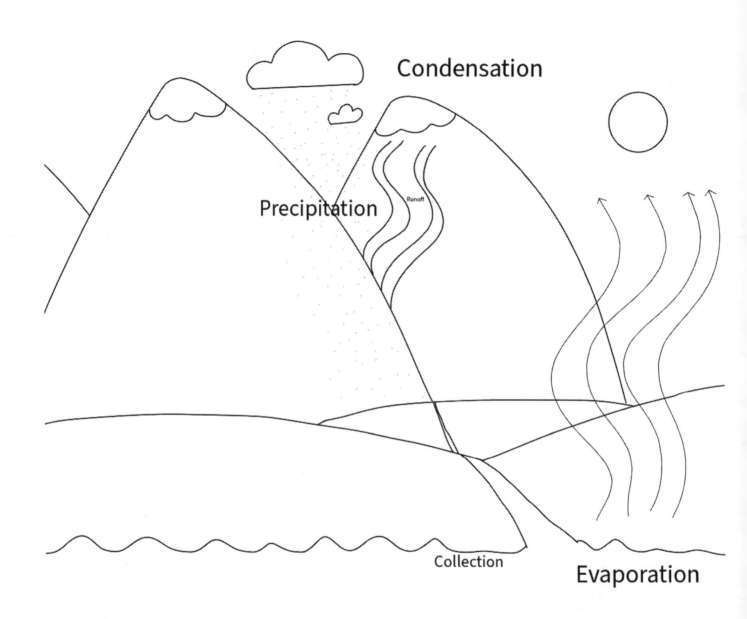

Condensation

Precipitation

Runoff

Collection

Evaporation

Investigating the Role of Atmospheric Particles on Cloud Formation

Objectives:
To investigate condensation with and without particulate surfaces to form on. Will spraying hairspray into the container effect the formation of condensation?

Materials:
- A clear cup or jar (Make sure the container can hold hot liquids. Avoid plastic or glass that cannot be heated. Pyrex measuring cups or mason jars are good options)
- Ice cubes
- A lid or plastic wrap
- Hairspray
- Hot water

Precautions:
Always wear protective equipment when performing science labs. This includes eye protection, gloves, and protective materials over your skin. This lab requires water be heated to high temperatures. Always exercise caution when dealing with hot liquid. Be cautious of spills and steam. When in doubt, ask a trusted adult for help.

Procedure:
1. Equip personal protection equipment.
2. Fill the container with hot water,
3. Carefully pour out 1/3 - 1/2 of the hot water.
4. Place the lid or plastic wrap over the container and stack a few ice cubes on top.
5. Observe and record your findings. After 5 minutes, empty the container.
6. Repeat steps 1-3.
7. Spray a quick spritz of hairspray into the container and cover quickly.
8. Place the ice onto the lid or plastic.
9. Observe what happens.
10. Take the lid off and see what comes out.

Analysis:
Analyze your data. What role did the hairspray play? Was there a difference between using hairspray and not using hairspray? What could you have done differently in this experiment? What can you conclude from this experiment? Was your hypothesis correct?

Thinking further:
Clouds are the formation of condensation droplets. But what does that condensation stick to? Did you ever notice the condensation in your bathroom after a bath clings to surfaces like the mirror? In the atmosphere, the water droplets condense onto particles of dust and aerosols. What do you think happens to the dust particles when it rains?

Earth Science Lab

Data Log

Earth Science Lab

Experiment Title:

Objective:

Hypothesis:

Procedure:

Observations/ Results:

Conclusion:

Earth Science Lab

Salt Water and Precipitation

Objectives:
To explore the process of evaporation, condensation, and precipitation of salt water. Will the salt evaporate with the water? Will it be rained down?

Materials:
- PPE
- Salt
- Water
- Stove
- Spoon
- Pan with fitting lid
- Mug
- Adult

Precautions:
Always wear protective equipment when performing science labs. This includes eye protection, gloves, and protective material over your skin. Ask an adult for supervision and guidance. Be cautious with hot water and steam. Both will burn you. Keep loose clothing, kitchen towels and mitts, and hair away from your heat source. When in doubt, ask a trusted adult for help.

Procedure:
1. Equip personal protection equipment.
2. Find an adult to help
3. Add 2 cups of warm water to the pan and mix in 2 teaspoons of salt until dissolved.
4. Making sure the water is not too hot to drink, take a small taste. Take note of the taste.
5. Next, with the help of an adult, place the pan on the stove with the lid on until the water comes to a boil. Turn off the burner.
6. Be cautious with this step. As condensation forms on the lid, remove the lid from the pan and allow the water to drip into the empty mug.
7. Let the water in the mug cool.
8. Once it is cooled, taste the water.
9. Note the taste.
10. Analyze your findings.

CONTINUED

Earth Science Lab

Analysis:

Analyze your data. What did you find? Were these results expected? How did the results compare to your hypothesis? What kind of environmental factors could change the results? What are your conclusions from performing the experiment?

Thinking Further:
Think about what this experiment represents in the water cycle. The ocean is made of salt water. As that water is heated and vaporized, does it take the salt along with it?
Research the vaporization points of water and sea salt. Does this explain your findings?

Earth Science Lab

Data Log

Earth Science Lab

Experiment Title:

Objective:

Hypothesis:

Procedure:

Observations/ Results:

Conclusion:

Earth Science Lab

The Greenhouse Effect

Fill in the blanks for this greenhouse effect diagram using the words from the word bank.

Sun
Atmosphere
Solar Radiation
Absorbed Radiation
Grennhouse Gases
Infrared Radiation
Re-radiated Energy

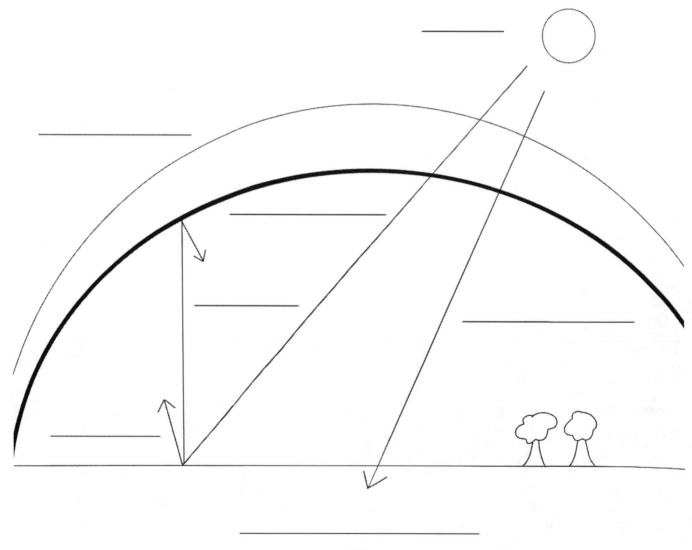

148

Greenhouse Effect

Observing the Greenhouse Effect

Objectives:

To investigate and observe temperatures in a container where the greenhouse effect is taking place vs one that is not. Will the covered container be hotter or colder than the uncovered container?

Materials:

- Two 2 Liter clear bottles with the tops cut off (Must be completely clear)
- Clear plastic wrap
- Two thermometers (Must fit inside the clear containers)
- A bright window or a place outside in direct light
- Soil
- Water

Precautions:

Always wear protective equipment when performing science labs. This includes eye protection, gloves, and protective materials over your skin. When in doubt, ask a trusted adult for help.

Procedure:

1. Equip personal protection equipment.
2. Fill each bottle about 1/3 full of soil. Make sure they are fairly equal.
3. Sprinkle some water into each bottle to make the soil damp.
4. Place a thermometer inside each bottle, propped up against the side so they can be easily read.
5. Cover one bottle with plastic wrap, tightly, making sure it is sealed properly.
6. Place both bottles in direct light. Make sure they are receiving equal amounts of light.
7. Observe both bottles once an hour for 3 hours. Record the temperature inside each bottle. Leave them overnight.
8. Check temperatures again the next morning and record.
9. Record the temperatures once more on day 3.
10. Analyze the data.

Analysis:

Analyze your data. What role did the plastic wrap play? Was there a difference between covering the bottle and not? What could you have done differently in this experiment? What can you conclude from this experiment? Was your hypothesis correct?

Thinking further:
Energy from the sun is absorbed into the objects on the Earth such as soil, oceans, houses, plants, etc. Those substances release some of the energy back into the atmosphere in the form of infrared radiation. In the atmosphere, the infrared radiation mixes with the greenhouse gases where it is re-radiated. What does this do for the Earth? Use this experiment to understand the role of the atmosphere on the temperature of the planet. Why is it an important process?

Earth Science Lab

Data Log

Earth Science Lab

Experiment Title:

Objective:

Hypothesis:

Procedure:

Observations/ Results:

Conclusion:

Earth Science Lab

Magnetism

Previously, we learned that rocks could be magnetic because the minerals that compose them have magnetic properties, but what does that mean?

Magnetism is caused by the motion of an electrical charge. The motion is caused by uneven electron distribution shifting the electrons' charge back and forth. These electrons move in patterns that are arranged in a manner in which they all spin in the same direction. The result of this charge is seen by objects either attracting or repelling each other.

You may have noticed that if you hold two **magnets**, or pieces of metal having magnetic properties, they can either push apart or come together, depending how you hold them. This is because of the **magnetic poles**. Each magnet has a north pole and a south pole (no penguins on either side, sorry). Holding two like poles together (north and north or south and south) will result in a repelling force between the two. And when the opposite poles are placed near each other, they produce an attracting force. But why?

There is an invisible field around a magnet called a **magnetic field**. The magnetic field is depicted here.

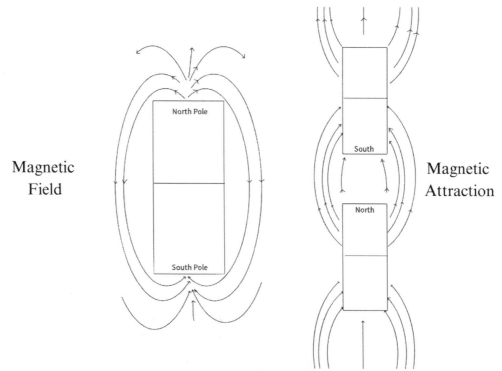

This field is where the force of magnetism is felt. It is depicted with **magnetic field lines**. These lines show the direction and strength of the magnetic field, bunching together where the field is strongest. If we study these lines, we can understand why placing two similar magnetic poles near each other would produce a repelling force.

Magnetism

We spoke before about certain objects holding a magnetic charge better than others. Iron and its ores are especially good at holding a magnetic charge. We call substances that are good at holding a magnetic charge **ferromagnetic**. Iron is ferromagnetic, as well as nickel and cobalt. These are naturally ferromagnetic.

We can also categorize magnetic metals into groups of metals that will stay magnetized for a long time and those that will easily lose their magnetism. Those that easily become demagnetized are called **magnetically soft** and those that stay magnetized for longer are called **magnetically hard**.

Search for metals that fit into the categories of ferromagnetic, magnetically hard, and magnetically soft. Do any metals fall into multiple categories?

Ferromagnetic	Magnetically Hard	Magnetically Soft

Magnetism

Magnetizing Metal

Objectives:
To observe whether or not magnetism can be transferred from one metal to another. Will stroking a bar magnet on a nail cause the nail to become magnetized?

Materials:
- PPE
- A large nail
- Loose staples, small paperclips, or similar objects
- Bar magnet

Precautions:
Always wear protective equipment when performing science labs. This includes eye protection, gloves, and protective materials over your skin. When in doubt, ask a trusted adult for help.

Procedure:
1. Equip personal protection equipment.
2. Place your loose staples, paperclips, etc. in a pile or in a shallow dish.
3. Touch the nail to the loose metal. Record your observations. What do you see? Do you observe any magnetic properties?
4. Take the bar magnet and rub it against the nail in one direction only, about 100 times.
5. Reat step 3. Do you observe any magnetism? If not, try rubbing the magnet on the nail in the same direction more than 100 times.
6. Analyze your findings.

Analysis:
Analyze your data. What happened in the interaction between the two metals? What could you have done differently in this experiment? What can you conclude from this experiment? Was your hypothesis correct?

Thinking further:
We know that magnetized metals have electrons that are all facing and spinning in the same direction. What do you think is happening as the magnet rubs against the nail? Why is it important to rub it in only one direction?

Earth Science Lab

Data Log

Experiment Title:

Objective:

Hypothesis:

Procedure:

Observations/ Results:

Conclusion:

Earth Science Lab

Solutions

Math

Page 3

Solution 1:

We are looking for two binomials whose product equals our quadratic expression $x^2 + 5x + 6$ We start by finding two numbers whose product is ac = 6 and whose sum is b = 5 (from the formula $ax^2+bx+c=0$). These numbers are 2 and 3. $2\times3= 6$, $2+3= 5$ $x^2 + 2x + 3x + 6$ $(x^2 +2x) + (3x + 6)$
$x(x + 2) + 3(x + 2)$ So, $(x+2)(x+3) = x^2 + 5x + 6$

Solution 2:

By carefully examining the expression, we can see that $x^2 - 4$ is actually a difference of squares, because it can be rewritten as $x^2 - 2^2$. So, we will use the difference of squares formula, $a^2 - b^2 = (a+b)(a-b)$ so, $(x+2)(x-2)$ Therefore, $x^2 - 4 = (x+2)(x-2)$

Solution 3:

For this problem, we will begin by finding the GCF of both 3 and 9. This number is 3. Therefore, $3x + 9$ becomes, $3(x + 3)$

Solution 4:

Again, we can find a greatest common factor for these numbers, which is 6, so our factored expression becomes $6(y - 2)$

Solution 5:

This is a simplified example of a time we can use factoring to solve a problem. We can find the number of rows by finding all the factors of 24 and then using the factor closest to 24. So we have: 1, 2, 3, 4, 6, 8, 12, 24 so Angela can arrange 12 figurines in each row to give her a total of 2 rows.

Page 4

Solution 6:

Looking to the quadratic form ax^2+bx+c, we will use the product-sum pattern to solve. We need to find two numbers whose product is ac and sum is b. ac = -30 and b = -7. The numbers in question are -10 and 3. So we will rewrite as: $2x^2 -10x+ 3x - 15$. Regroup with common factors: $(2x^2 + 3x) + (-10x - 15)$ $x(2x + 3) - 5(2x + 3)$ which simplifies to $(x - 5)(2x + 3)$

Solution 7:

ac = 24, b = 10 so $3x^2 + 6x + 4x + 8$ and group $(3x^2 +6x) + (4x+8)$ $3x(x +2) + 4(x+2)$ so our factors are $(3x + 4)(x + 2)$

158

Math

Page 4

Solution 8:

First, factor out the negative. $-1(6x^2 + x - 2)$ $ac = 12$ $b = 1$ so $-(6x^2 + 4x - 3x - 2)$

$-((6x^2 + 4x) + (-3x - 2))$ becomes $-(2x(3x + 2) - (3x + 2))$ so factored form is: $-(2x - 1)(3x + 2)$

Solution 9:

$x^2 + 4x - 77$ $x^2 + 11x - 7x - 77$ $(x^2 + 11x) - (7x + 77)$ $x(x + 11) - 7(x + 11)$

$(x - 7)(x + 11)$

Page 5

Solution 10:

Area of a rectangle = Length × Width. We have two equations for area: $L = 3 + 2w$ and $L \times W = 90$. We will plug in the value of L from the first equation into the second so: $(3 + 2w) \times w = 90$ or $3w + 2w^2 = 90$ rearrange and set to 0: $2w^2 + 3w - 90 = 0$ Now factor $(2w + 15)(w - 6) = 0$ so $w = -7.5$ or $w = 6$ We will choose the positive value to plug into $L \times W = 90$ so $L \times 6 = 90$ $L = 15$ Therefore $L = 15$ m $W = 6$ m

Solution 11:

$ac = -18$, $b = -7$, so $3x^2 + 2x - 9x - 6$ and $(3x^2 + 2x) - (9x + 6)$ so $x(3x + 2) - 3(3x + 2)$ therefore $(x - 3)(3x + 2)$

Solution 12:

$x^2 + 6x + 9$ which is $x^2 + 3x + 3x + 9$ regroup $(x^2 + 3x) + (3x + 9)$ so $x(x + 3) + 3(x + 3)$ therefore the factored form is $(x + 3)(x + 3)$

Solution 13:

$10x^2 + 13x - 3$ is $10x^2 + 15x - 2x - 3$ so $(10x^2 + 15x) - (2x + 3)$ which is $5x(2x + 3) - (2x + 3)$ so the factored form is $(5x - 1)(2x + 3)$

Math

Page 6

Solution 14:

a. Leading term, b. Degree, c. Coefficients, d. Constant

Solution 15:

You should have circled all of the options. These are all examples of polynomials. Polynomials can have one term (monomials), two terms (binomials), three terms (trinomials), or more (multinomial).

Solution 16:

$(2x+4)(5x^2+2x-3)$ Multiply both of the terms in the binomial with each term in the trinomial to get: $10x^3+4x^2-6x+20x^2+8x-12$ then combine like terms $10x^3+24x^2+2x-12$

Page 7

Solution 17:

A rational expression is a ratio of two polynomials or a fraction whose numerator and denominator are both polynomials; they are especially helpful in solving problems of rate and time.

Solution 18:

First we will factor anything in the numerator or denominator that can be factored.

$\dfrac{(x-2)(x+2)}{x-2}$ Now cancel common factors $\dfrac{(\cancel{x-2})(x+2)}{\cancel{x-2}}$ so we get x+2 where x≠ 2

Solution 19:

Factor where possible $\dfrac{(x-3)(x+3)}{x-3}$ $\dfrac{(\cancel{x-3})(x+3)}{\cancel{x-3}}$ x+3 where x≠ 3

Solution 20:

Find a common factor $\dfrac{(x^2+2x+4)(x-2)}{(x-2)(x-2)}$ $\dfrac{x^2+2x+4}{x-2}$ where x≠2

Math

Page 8

Solution 21:

$(3x^2-5x^2) + (2x+4x) + (-2-7) = -2x^2+6x-9$

Solution 22:

$(2a-4a) + (3b + 5b) + (C) - (6) = -2a+8b+c-6$

Solution 23:

Distribute first. $3x + 15 + 2x - 8$ simplify $5x + 7$

Solution 24:

Distribute first. $2x + 6 - 14x + 35$ simplify $-12x + 41$

Solution 25:

$6x + 8 - 4x + 10 + 6x^2 + 6x$ simplify $6x^2 + 8x + 18$

Page 9

Solution 26:

Rule for multiplying with different exponents with the same base: $a\char`\^m \times a\char`\^n = a\char`\^m+n$

so $2^3 \times 2^2$ we add the exponents $3+2=5$ so $2^5= 32$

Solution 27:

$9\times9= 81$ so $\sqrt{81} = 9$

Solution 28:

Rule for multiplying with exponents when bases are different but powers are the same: $a\char`\^m \times b\char`\^m = (a\times b)\char`\^m$ so $2^3 \times 3^3 = (2\times3) = 6$ so $6^3 = 216$

Math

Solution 29:

Rule for multiplying with exponents when the bases and the powers are different: $a\string^m \times b\string^n = (a\string^m) \times (b\string^n)$ so $2^3 \times 4^2 = 8 \times 16 = 128$

Solution 30:

$(3x^2)^3$ is the same as $(3)^3 \times (x^2)^3 = 27 \times x^6 = 27x^6$

Solution 31:

$\sqrt{225} = 25$ and $\sqrt{16} = 4$ so $25 + 4 = 29$

Solution 32:

First multiply the coefficients $4 \times 19 = 76$ then combine the exponents since both bases are x so x^5 answer: $76x^5$

Solution 33:

First distribute the exponent $(19)^5$ and $(x^3)^5$ $19^5 = 2,476,099$ and because we have a power of a power we multiply the powers so $3 \times 5 = 15$ Therefore our answer is $2,476,009x^{15}$

Solution 34:

First distribute the exponent $(5)^2$ and $(x^3)^2$ $5^2 = 25$ and we multiply powers of powers to get x^6 so we get $25x^6$

Solution 35:

We will first place this division problem into fraction form $\dfrac{4x^2}{2}$ and then cancel like terms from the numerator and denominator which is 2. So we get $\dfrac{2x^2}{1}$ or $2x^2$

Math

Page 10

Solution 36:

$y = mx + b$

Solution 37:

$y = mx + b$ y = dependent variable, m = line slope, x = independent variable, b = y-intercept

Solution 38:

$m = \dfrac{rise}{run}$ $m = \dfrac{y_2 - y_1}{x_2 - x_1}$

Solution 39:

$y - y_1 = m(x - x_1)$

Solution 40:

Slope-intercept form is the equation of a straight line. It gives you the slope in the form of rise/run and the y-intercept that the line passes through. This is the most convenient equation to use for graphing a line. Point-slope form can be used to find the equation of a line when you are given a point by which the line passes through (that is not the y-intercept) and the slope.

Page 11

Solution 41:

Because the line passes through the point (0, 0), there will be no b in this equation. We will have a slope of 3 so $y = 3x$.

Solution 42:

Because our line passes through the point (0,1), our y intercept (b) = 1. Slope or m, is equal to change in y/ change in x. Here our slope is negative because as x increases, y decreases. So we have $y = (-3/4)x + 1$.

Math

Solution 43:

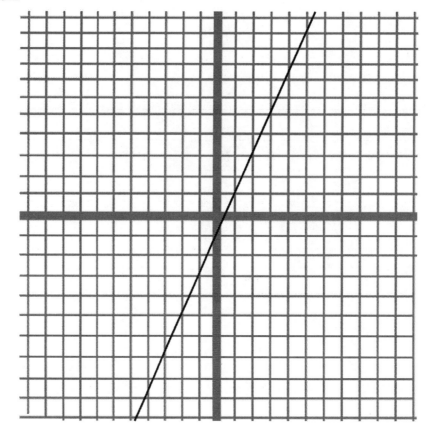

Solution 44:

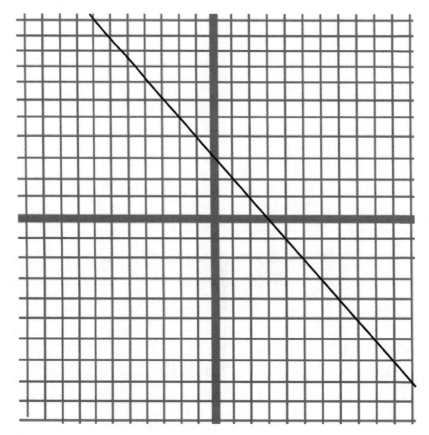

Math

Solution 45:

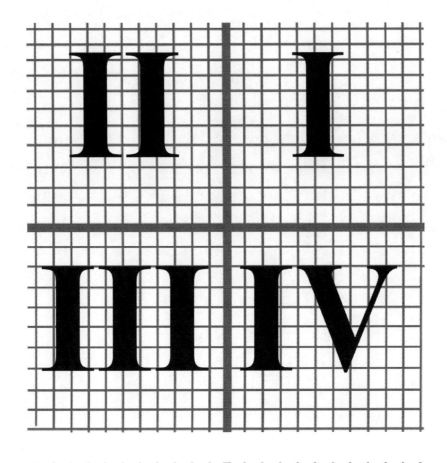

Solution 46:

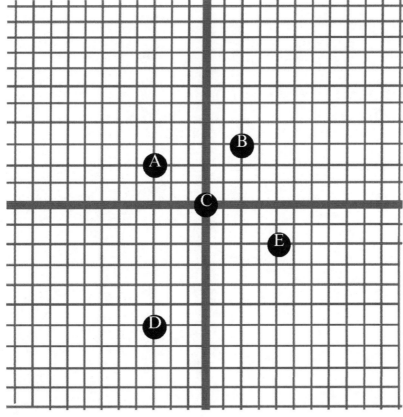

Math

Page 14

Solution 47:

First, we multiply the number of bags per day by 7 to get pounds per week. $4.5 \times 7 = 31.5$ lbs per week. Now we multiply that by 3 weeks to get 94.5 lbs in 3 weeks. Now we must divide the total pounds used by the pounds in each bag to get total bags needed, which is $94.5/10 = 9.45$ bags. Since we can't buy partial bags, the restaurant will need to purchase 10 bags for 3 weeks.

Solution 48:

To find the area of a rectangle, we use the formula, $a = L \times W$ so $90 \times 1200 = 108{,}000$. The answer to this formula is always in square units, and since we are working with feet our answer is $108{,}000 \text{ ft}^2$ (2.48 acres or 1 hectare)

Solution 49:

$x + y = 107$

$x - y = 75$

Use substitution. $x = y + 75$ so $(y + 75) + y = 107$ $2y = 32$ $y = 32/2$ $y = 16$ now place y to find the value of x. $x + (16) = 107$ $x = 91$

Vocabulary

Page 36

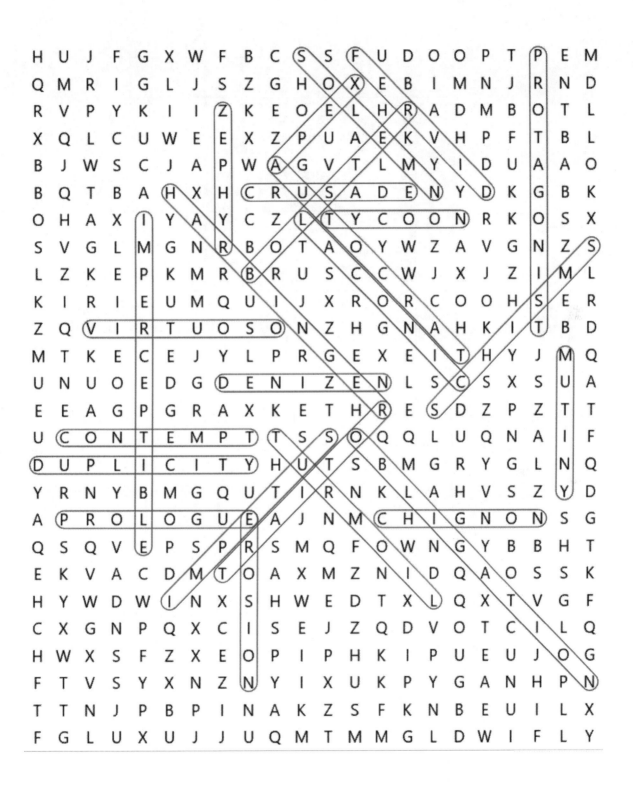

H U J F G X W F B C S S F U D O O P T P E M
Q M R I G L J S Z G H O X E B I M N J R N D
R V P Y K I I Z K E O E L H R A D M B O T L
X Q L C U W E E X Z P U A E K V H P F A B L
B J W S C J A P W A G V T L M Y I D U A A O
B Q T B A H X H C R U S A D E N Y D K G B K
O H A X I Y A Y C Z L T Y C O O N R K O S X
S V G L M G N R B O T A O Y W Z A V G N Z S
L Z K E P K M R B R U S C C W J X J Z I M L
K I R I E U M Q U I J X R O R C O O H S E R
Z Q V I R T U O S O N Z H G N A H K I T B D
M T K E C E J Y L P R G E X E I T H Y J M Q
U N U O E D G D E N I Z E N L S C S X S U A
E E A G P G R A X K E T H R E S D Z P Z T T
U C O N T E M P T T S S O Q Q L U Q N A I F
D U P L I C I T Y H U T S B M G R Y G L N Q
Y R N Y B M G Q U T I R N K L A H V S Z Y D
A P R O L O G U E A J N M C H I G N O N S G
Q S Q V E P S P R S M Q F O W N G Y B B H T
E K V A C D M T O A X M Z N I D Q A O S S K
H Y W D W I N X S H W E D T X L Q X T V G F
C X G N P Q X C I S E J Z Q D V O T C I L Q
H W X S F Z X E O P I P H K I P U E U J O G
F T V S Y X N Y I X U K P Y G A N H P N
T T N J P B B P I N A K Z S F K N B E U I L X
F G L U X U J J U Q M T M M G L D W I F L Y

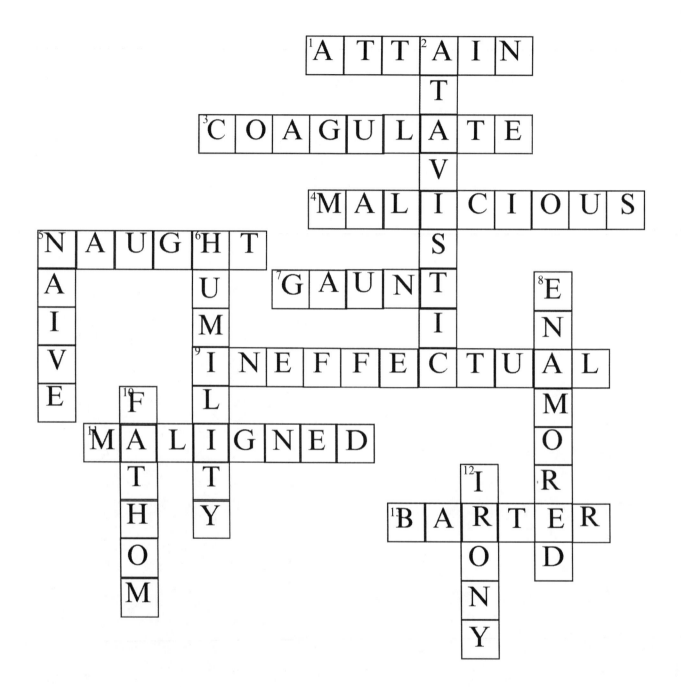

Writing

Page 69

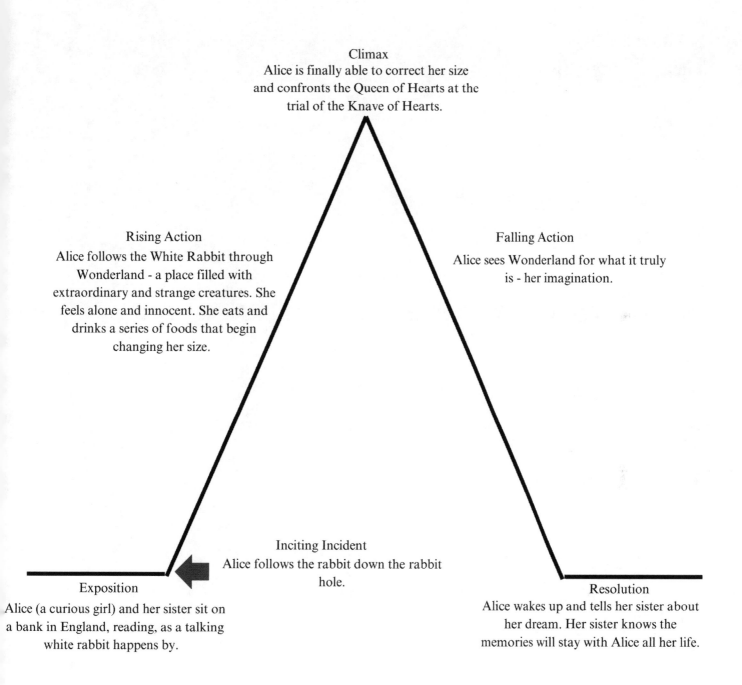

Climax
Alice is finally able to correct her size
and confronts the Queen of Hearts at the
trial of the Knave of Hearts.

Rising Action
Alice follows the White Rabbit through
Wonderland - a place filled with
extraordinary and strange creatures. She
feels alone and innocent. She eats and
drinks a series of foods that begin
changing her size.

Falling Action
Alice sees Wonderland for what it truly
is - her imagination.

Inciting Incident
Alice follows the rabbit down the rabbit
hole.

Exposition
Alice (a curious girl) and her sister sit on
a bank in England, reading, as a talking
white rabbit happens by.

Resolution
Alice wakes up and tells her sister about
her dream. Her sister knows the
memories will stay with Alice all her life.

History

Solution 1:

The 15th Century CE

Solutuin 2:

The 1st Century BCE

Solution 3:

The 20th Century CE

Solution 4:

The 15th Century CE

Solution 5:

The 16th Century CE

Solution 6:

The 17th Century CE

Solution 7:

The 19th Century CE

Solution 8:

The 21st Century CE

Solution 9:

The 18th Century CE

Solution 10:

The 2nd Century BCE

History

Page 85

ANSWERS WILL VARY but can include the following countries which have been these types of governments at some point in their history

Aristocracy: Nigeria, The United Kingdom, Denmark, Russia

Communist: China, Cambodia, Cuba, The Soviet Union

Monarchy: Saudi Arabia, Belgium, Grenada, Japan

Democracy: Switzerland, The United States, Greece, Denmark

Federalist: Australia, Brazil, The United States

Totalitarian: Germany, The USSR, Italy, Japan

Oligarchy: Ukraine, Iran, Russia

History

Important points about Ancient Egypt:

The fall of Ancient Egypt was a slow decline over several centuries, largely due to multiple reasons, including political, social, and environmental factors. Here are some issues they faced:

- Political instability after political fragmentation followed the New Kingdom period. Civil wars and a weakened central authority resulted. This, coupled with less effective rulers led to political instability.
- Invasions by Assyrian, Persian, Roman, and Macedonian forces caused severe damages and caused the Egyptian rule to end in the area. Egypt eventually became a Roman province.
- Societal issues were a large challenge for the area, stemming from long-term economic difficulties from loss of trade routes and drought. Outside influences from Greek and Roman cultures also eroded Egyptian traditions.
- Natural challenges also played a role in the challenges Egyptians faced, The Nile River being a vital part of living, caused issues with its variability. Flooding and drought were harder to handle with an unstable economy and weak leadership.

Important points about Mesoamerica:

- Politics: The Aztecs were ruled by an emperor in a hierarchical society. Their capital was on an isle in Texcoco. The Incans had a theocracy run by a monarchy in Cusco. The Mayans had decentralized city-states in which each city-state had its own king.
- Religion: Each civilization was polytheistic with their own gods. They all worshipped with sacrifice, sometimes including human sacrifice.
- Achievements: The Aztecs had great engineering achievements including floating gardens, large cities, and temples. They also had pictographic writing and a calendar system. The Incas had extensive road networks and agriculture. They also invented a system for record keeping with knotted strings. The Mayans had glyphs and sophisticated astronomical knowledge. They are credited with developing the concept of 0 and creating an accurate calendar.
- Geography: AZTEC: Central Mexico, fertile lands and lakes. INCA: Andes Mountains, diverse environments. MAYA: Southern Mexico and Central America, tropical.
- Decline: Both the Incas and Aztecs were conquered by the Spanish in the 1500's. The Mayans declined in the 800's because of warfare, environmental factors, and drought.

Important points about European Exploration:

- Christopher Columbus is often credited with discovering the Americas in 1492 (though we have a lot of evidence suggesting many others landed there first). However, his voyages did lead to a widespread awareness of the Americas in Europe and a resurgence of interest in colonizing it. Spain funded these voyages.
- Ferdinand Magellan was credited to be the first to circumnavigate the globe (1519-1522), seemingly resolving the globe/flat earth debate and that all the oceans are connected. This gave a better understanding of global geography. He was also funded by Spain.
- Amerigo Vespucci voyaged (1497-1504) along the coast of South America to establish that the Americas were not actually Asia as Columbus suspected, but a new continent. He was funded by Spain and then Portugal.
- Economic interests are an obvious motivator in the exploration of the world at this time. New trade routes would help access foreign commodities and also help in warfare and increasing political influence. Spreading the influence of the Catholic church was another great motivator for the Spanish.
- Destruction and displacement were effects the indigenous peoples faced by European conquest. Disease and warfare would mar the populations. Exploitation and cultural erosion were major factors in the decline of these civilizations.
- Global trade, colonization, and the influence of the Catholic church have effects that have lasted until this day

172

History

Important points about Joan of Arc:

She was born in 1412 in France. She was a peasant who claimed she had visions and heard voices from saints instructing her to support Charles VII so as to help drive the English out of France. At 17 years old, she convinced Charles VII to allow her to lead an army to lift the Siege of Orleans, changing the course of the 100 Years' War. The English later put her on trial for heresy and witchcraft. She was found guilty and burned at the stake in 1431, age 19, solidifying her role as a martyr for France. After her death, she was retried and cleared of all charges. Joan showed unwavering faith and courage, even against gender barriers and age. She showed that one person's conviction could change the course of history.

Important points about the Dark Ages:

- The classes included nobility and clergy, knights, peasants and serfs, and merchants.
- Nobles lived in castles where they wore clothing made of silks and fur even more elaborate than today's garments. They received education in military training, manners, and literacy. They had power but were often threatened by warfare. Clergy lived in monasteries and on land owned by the church, and they wore more plain clothing such as robes. Their main education was in theology, philosophy, and literacy. They also learned music; however, they were restricted in worldly activities. Both groups had access to high quality foods.
- Knights resided in castles or manors provided by their lords. They were provided armor and wore other clothing suitable for battle. They ate a diet heavy in meats and grains. Their education focused on combat training and horsemanship, but they sometimes learned manners and literacy. They obviously faced the dangers of battle, but they also had the ability to advance through military prowess and networking.
- Peasants lived in simple huts and wore clothing made of wool or linen. They ate mainly grains, vegetables, and dairy, with limited meats. Very few in this class had access to education, but they did learn family trades. They lived with harsh working conditions and were heavily taxed. Social mobility was limited.
- Merchants lived in sturdier housing with varied clothing, nicer than serfs. They had access to more food because of trade networks. Some could afford education. They faced the danger of banditry but had better opportunity for wealth and social mobility.

Important points about Castles:

- Castles were strategically placed on elevated terrain for natural defense reasons. They were typically built in compact, irregular shapes adapting to the contours of the land.
- Walls were thick, made of stone or brick, and could withstand severe damages. Towers were placed for archers and lookouts.
- Drawbridges and gateways were often used.
- The central keep housed the lords and served as the last line of defense.
- Castles served as military defense, economic centers, symbols of power, and places of political authority.
- Castles are often romanticized today but are still seen as symbols of power and authority. They are admired on an architectural level.

Important points about Printing Presses:

- This new press allowed for rapid and efficient printing using movable type, which led to mass production and more affordable and accessible texts.
- Knowledge and information could be more easily spread. Printed books helped standardize spellings and grammar, which led to the development of national languages.
- This press helped accelerate developments that contributed to the transition from midieval to early modern era.

History

Important points about the Protestant Reformation:

The Protestant reformation largely came about due to dissatisfaction by Christians of the mandated state religion of the Catholic church and what they perceived to be false doctrine imposed on the people. The Catholic church would put to death any who disobeyed the laws of the state-run religion. Reformers believed the teachings were unbiblical and wished to worship in a way they believed to be Biblically founded. For example, infant baptism was a point of contention. The printing press allowed Luther's theses to be more easily spread. The people were under economic stress while the church seemed to be flourishing. This was another point of contention for the people being controlled by the church. Many branches of Christianity stemmed from this movement and continue to exist today.

Important points about the Ming Dynasty:

Lanscape paintings became very popular during this time. The creation of the kiln fostered the love for white and blue ceramics. Opera became popular, and the creation of Chinese vernacular language offered more accessible reading for average readers. Economic stability and growth allowed for less stress and more time for hobbies and arts. Public schooling allowed for more students to receive an education.

Important points about 16th Century Russia:

Ivan the terrible ruled over Russia from 1547 - 1584. He expanded the territory and instated a centralized authority with the title Tsar. The tsar was supreme leader over nobility and regions. Serfs were heavily taxed and were not seeing prosperity or mobility. They faced many economic challenges such as poverty and overcrowding in urban areas. Ivan's policies paved the way for later autocratic rule. Orthodox Christianity influenced the culture and Russian society. This period saw great territorial expansion and political centralization, which would ultimately help the upper class while subduing the lower classes. This would lay the groundwork for future autocracy which defined Russia's history for centuries.

Important points about the New World colonies:

Spain claimed areas that are now lower USA and Mexico (think Florida, Texas, and California). They sought wealth and the spread of the Catholic church. France claimed areas around the St. Lawrence River and the Mississippi River in modern day Canada and the USA. They were heavily involved in fur trades with Native Americans. England settled the East Coast and sought economic opportunities as well as religious freedom. Africans were already widely traded as slaves in Africa and were forcibly brought to the Carribean and the America mainland to work large farms. English, Scottish, and Irish citizens entered contracts as payment for passage to America. These were indentured slaves. They sometimes earned land or money at the end of the contract. This was different than forced slavery. Natives were used as slaves early on, but their lack of resistance to European diseases made them less desirable than Africans, who were seen as more resilient. Food shortages, war with natives, and sickness were dangers settlers were willing to face for their travels to whichever promise in hope they believed in.

Important points about the Spanish conquest:

There were severe military conflicts between the indigenous people and conquistadores. There were resistance efforts by natives, but they were eventually suppressed. Natives also faced disease, forced labor, and cultural suppression. The exploitation of natives is what often stands out as a stark difference to military conquest in European nations at the time as well as the impact on the native cultures which contrasted so much to European culture.

Science

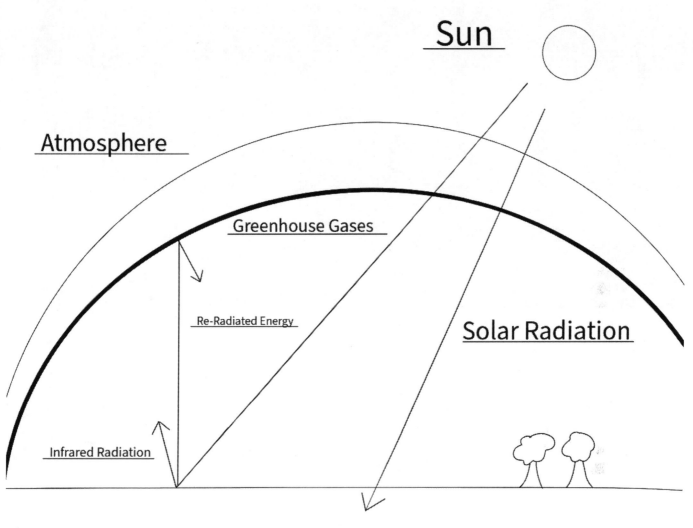

Sun

Atmosphere

Greenhouse Gases

Re-Radiated Energy

Solar Radiation

Infrared Radiation

Absorbed Energy

Made in the USA
Las Vegas, NV
18 October 2024